Ancient-Future
WORSHIP

Ancient-Future

WORSHIP

Proclaiming and Enacting God's Narrative

Robert E. Webber

BakerBooks
a division of Baker Publishing Group
Grand Rapids, Michigan

Published by Baker Books
a division of Baker Publishing Group
P.O. Box 6287, Grand Rapids, MI 49516-6287
www.bakerbooks.com

Second printing, October 2008

Printed in the United States of America

Library of Congress Cataloging-in-Publication Data
Webber, Robert.
    Ancient-future worship : proclaiming and enacting God's narrative / Robert E. Webber.
       p.   cm.
    Includes bibliographical references (p.   ).
    ISBN 978-0-8010-6624-5 (pbk.)
    1. Public worship. I. Title.
BV15.W383 2008
264—dc22   2007045153

In keeping with biblical principles of creation stewardship, Baker Publishing Group advocates the responsible use of our natural resources. As a member of the Green Press Initiative, our company uses recycled paper when possible. The text paper of this book is comprised of 30% post-consumer waste.

Ancient-Future Worship is lovingly dedicated to
my children, their spouses, my grandchildren,
and a few select pets.

John and Isabel Webber
Natalie and Raquel

Alexandra and Jack Wilson
Quinn

Stefany and Tom Welch
Tommy, Jack, Ben, Lexie

Jeremy and Susie Buffam
their dogs, Condi and The Gipper

I have always loved you in life,
and I will love you still in death.

Contents

Foreword

Bob Webber: Memory and Hope

The following tribute was presented at the Wheaton College Theology Conference banquet in April 2007 and later presented via videotape to Bob Webber, who was unable to attend. The conference theme, "Ancient Faith for the Church's Future," was one of the central motifs in Robert Webber's writings. Webber died the following week.

*D*ear Robert,
Two of life's best gifts are memory and hope. This is true in psalmody and eucharistic praying but also in personal and professional friendship. It is a great honor to practice both of these gifts with respect to your life and work, especially here at Wheaton College.

When I think of your written and published works, I remember with deep gratitude opening up *Worship Is a Verb* at about age eighteen and feeling an Emmaus-like burning of the heart over its conviction about our risen Lord and its catholic vision for worship.

Publisher's Note: Bob Webber's passion for what he termed an "ancient-future faith" had an evangelistic impact over the years on many students and readers, especially in contemporary church worship circles. The following tribute sets Bob's contributions in perspective and was delivered just prior to his death in 2007. For this his last book in the Ancient-Future series we thought this remembrance to be a fitting foreword to *Ancient-Future Worship*. May Bob's ministry and legacy live on through these pages.

Some years later, I remember receiving seven boxes of files, which became the last volumes of the Complete Library of Christian Worship, and sensing the breadth of the landscape that you explored—the whole Bible, all of systematic theology, two thousand years of church history, every one of the church's various ministries, in one hundred or more denominations (all, it seemed, in a single summer). Later, I remember arriving at a hotel in Carol Stream on Monday to learn that we would be starting and finishing our outline of the *Renew* songbook in four days. I remember how you said then (and many times since), "I love a project."

As I think about all of your published work, I am struck by some particular charisms that you have shared so freely with us.

First, you have introduced so many of us to the early church as a period of unique theological insight, spiritual vitality, and prophetic correction. You did so in a way that energized practicing pastors and lay Christians. It was said of Princeton's Peter Brown, "He rescued the past from the tyranny of stereotypes." That is also true for you, especially when it comes to worship.

Part of your work has been simply to get us up to speed with a new set of terms. You taught us that *epiphany* and *Eucharist* are useful terms. You taught us to pronounce *epiclesis, anamnesis,* and *Hippolytus*. You also exercised restraint, sparing us the frustration of feeling that we had to use the words *catechumenate* and *mystagogy* when all we wanted to do was lead people on a *Journey to Jesus*.

You also coined phrases about our emerging love for the early church, leading the way as "blended" worship became "convergence" worship and then "ancient-future" worship. Many publishers wanted to know what you were calling it—a sign that you were not only describing a movement but shaping it.

In all of these projects, you were especially adept at writing for people with little previous exposure to the material, a pedagogical skill very much undervalued in the academy. So often when writing reaches out to broad audiences, it ceases to be compelling. But I've found that people who read your material actually end up learning things, rather than simply having their prior assumptions confirmed.

Part of your skill is your ability to map big stretches of territory (historically, conceptually, geographically), never letting us miss the forest for the trees. Your most recent book, *The Divine Embrace: Recovering the Passionate Spiritual Life,* gathers the fruit of a lifetime of teaching this material in congregations. You've chosen a set of the most crucial themes for promoting vibrant Christian faith and life, and you pursue them doggedly. Some of your many students will later come along to study the leaves on some of the trees in the forests you describe. But I hope they do not forget that a map of the big picture is vitally important for the life of the church.

Second, you did not shrink back from honest criticism and polemic. Like Irenaeus, you have been "against heresies." Providentially, you have been against some of the same ones he was against.

Reading your work again this winter, I have been struck by the multiple objects of your published indignation: spirit-matter dualism, ahistorical mysticism, experientialism, legalism, romanticism, narcissism, "McSpirituality," privatism, Gnosticism, and love songs to Jesus. You reserved equal ink to protest intellectualism and anti-intellectualism. You even put your feelings in your titles, giving us a 1984 *Christianity Today* article, "Let's Put Worship into the Worship Service: Let's End Gospel Pep Rallies and Sunday Morning Variety Shows," a 1985 book *Secular Humanism: Threat and Challenge*, and a 1999 article in *Leadership*, "Reducing God to Music? We Experience God in More Than Songs and Segues." Indeed, the Chicago Call uses the locution "we deplore" five times.

We knew that even when you criticized us, you loved us. The twinkle in your eye gave you away. And so did your ability to see both sides of complex issues. You embraced tensions and pulled us back from unnecessary polarities, calling us to both social justice and personal transformation, both hand-clapping exuberance and profound introspection, both restless yearning for change and a profound gratitude for the inheritance of faith. You called us to both truth and passion.

You are one of the few writers who, despite a convert's zeal, could have the poise to end *Evangelicals on the Canterbury Trail: Why Evangelicals Are Attracted to the Liturgical Church* with a section titled "Evangelical Contribution to Canterbury: What Evangelicals Bring to the Liturgical Tradition."

Third, your writings have taught us how teachers can helpfully work at several levels at the same time. You wrote books for classrooms, continuing education events, and small groups. When evangelicals got excited about this or that genre, your entrepreneurial instincts unfailingly seized the opportunity, giving us inductive Bible studies, a songbook, textbooks, ecumenical call statements, family prayer books, and newsletters. When we wanted a prayer book, you published *Prymer*. When we wanted pilgrimage stories, you offered *Evangelicals on the Canterbury Trail*. When we told you how much we loved paradigms, you delivered the goods, giving us *The Younger Evangelicals*. When we said you needed to write a dissertation on someone like William Perkins, you complied, writing about how much he loved the early church. When Donald Bloesch, Donald Dayton, Peter Gillquist, Thomas Howard, Richard Lovelace, and Roger Nicole were all still trying to get published back in the 1970s, you helped to organize them, giving us the Chicago Call. Indeed, like parents who struggle to help their toddler eat healthy food, you knew your audience. You offered us the protein of embodied, *Christus Victor*, missional, sacramental Christianity in every way possible.

I recall vividly that in the last year of his life, James F. White, one of the leading Methodist liturgical historians of the twentieth century, was campaigning for you to receive the North American Academy of Liturgy's Berakah lifetime achievement award, recognizing what an accomplishment all of this was. Yet what Jim never came to know was the genre of writing that for me is among the most profound: the update emails you and Joanne have sent over the past six months. In the face of cancer, these short notes have offered us a testimony of profound faith, honest lament, and resilient, resurrection hope. These emails are a symbol of a final feature of your work.

Best of all, your writings have testified to the gospel of Jesus, the beauty of the Triune God, and the deep joy of a full-orbed Christian life. The Orthodox teach us never to look *at* icons but rather to look *through* them. And we know that the best way to receive your books is not simply to analyze them but to see through them.

And when we do, what do we see?

A God who acts in history by Word and Spirit.

A sturdy affirmation: "Christ has died, Christ is risen, Christ will come again."

A cross that offers not only forgiveness but also healing.
A Spirit who sanctifies not only our minds but our bodies.
Baptism that not only washes us but drowns us.
A meal that not only looks back but also looks forward.

And that is what we also do now. For as nourishing as memory is, hope is even better. So in resolute hope, we promise to do so much of what you called us to: remember our baptism, pray in the Spirit, flee to the Eucharist.

This Eastertide, we claim again the promise of our baptism, joining our voices to that of Scripture and all the saints who declare:

> Blessed be the God and Father of our Lord Jesus Christ! By his great mercy we have been born anew to a living hope through the resurrection of Jesus Christ from the dead, and to an inheritance which is imperishable, undefiled, and unfading, kept in heaven for you, who by God's power are guarded through faith for a salvation ready to be revealed in the last time.
>
> 1 Peter 1:3–5 RSV

In Christian hope,

John Witvliet
April 10, 2007

Acknowledgments

I have become keenly aware of what a privilege it is to be an author since being diagnosed with terminal pancreatic cancer on August 25, 2006. During the writing of this, my final book, I have taken time to think back over my thirty years of writing and reflect on numerous books, people, and events that have shaped my content and style. I have also thankfully considered the many opportunities to respond to the church's situation in this culture and the publishers who have so graciously supported me in the publication of my writings.

My major publisher since 1999 has been Baker Books. I particularly want to thank Bob Hosack, the senior editor. He first approached me about republishing *Common Roots* (originally published in 1978). The republished work became *Ancient-Future Faith* (1999) and led ultimately into the present Ancient-Future series. During these years Bob Hosack has become more than an editor. We have spent time with his family in our home, on the beach, and in many restaurants. Thank you, Bob, for your professional support and for your personal relationship. Both have meant much to me. A special word of thanks also to Paul Brinkerhoff and Lois Stück for their careful editing.

It was just about the same time that Bob Hosack and I began to work together that Northern Seminary offered me the William R. and Geraldyne B. Myers Chair of Ministry. I left Wheaton College in 2000 to begin this appointment. Because of the reduced teaching load, I was able to have more time for writing. Then, after six years of teaching I was granted a sabbatical (June 2006 to April 2007). It was during this time I was able to write this book.

I owe a tremendous debt of gratitude to Northern Seminary for all they have done for me. These past seven years are full of happy Northern memories—the administration, staff, faculty, students, and board of trustees have been a marvelous group of people to work with. The sense of community at various levels of academe, spiritual, and personal relationships has been challenging, inspiring, and always supportive.

At the same time—once again—when I started at Northern, my former student and friend, Ashley Gieschen, joined me as my administrative assistant. During the seven years Ashley has been the key person in transmitting my ideas and projects from the spoken word to the written word. She was the one who sat at the computer forever typing draft after draft of the nine books produced in those years. In all that time there was never a word of complaint from Ashley—only an overwhelming enthusiasm for her work and a sense of joy at everything we produced together. In all these ways Ashley has been a true friend, a kindred spirit, and a genuine spiritual mentor.

I cannot leave this earthly scene without highlighting the key role played in my last seven years of ministry by Northern Seminary, Bob Hosack and Baker Books, and Ashley Gieschen. Without them, this and the other books written during this period of time would not have been completed.

And what can I say about my dear wife? I cannot find the words to express the gratitude I have toward her love for me shown in her support of my schedule for the past seven years. I was sixty-six when I retired from Wheaton in 2000. Most retirees look forward to travel, visits with the grandchildren, and a more relaxed pace of life. Not me. I said, "My life and my ministry are one. I want to live, teach, and write until I die." Joanne's support has been unequivocal. And in the last seven months of my life, she turned her hands and feet into the hands and feet of Jesus. She served me with her love to the very end, making sure I was comfortable and out of pain as much as possible. As often as she could she sat with me by the fireplace to write. And so I did, completing this manuscript only weeks before my death.

Finally, I should say a word of thanks to you—my reader. Books cannot be written and published without readers. And so you, too, have made it possible for me to write. Through the years many of you have interacted with me at conferences, via the phone, and through email. I hope I responded to you with the sense of responsibility and gratitude I feel in my heart toward my readers.

Thank you—everyone—for opening so many doors and for walking through the doors with me step by step, day by day.

Robert E. Webber
Lent 2007

Introduction to the Ancient-Future Series

*T*his book, *Ancient-Future Worship*, belongs to the Ancient-Future series. In each book of the series I present an issue related to faith and Christian practice from a particular point of view, namely, that of drawing wisdom from the past and translating these insights into the present and future life of the church, its faith, worship, ministry, and spirituality.

In these books I address current issues in the context of three very significant quests taking place in the church today. First, these books speak to the longing to discover the roots of the faith in the biblical and classical tradition of the church. I affirm the Bible as the final authority in all matters of faith and practice. Instead of disregarding the developments of faith in the church, however, I draw on the foundational interpretation of the church fathers and the creeds and practices of the ancient church. These are sources in which Christian truth has been summarized and articulated over against heretical teaching.

Second, this series is committed to the current search for unity in the church. Therefore, I draw from the entire history of the church together with its many manifestations—Orthodox, Catholic, and Protestant—particularly the Reformers and evangelicals like John Wesley and Jonathan Edwards. I weave insights from these traditions into the text so the reader will understand how other deeply committed Christians have sought to think and live the faith in other places and times.

Finally, I use these biblical, ancient roots together with insights and practices from Christian history to constitute the foundation for addressing the third issue faced by today's church: How do you deliver the authentic faith and great wisdom of the past into the new cultural situation of the twenty-first century? The way into the future, I argue, is not an innovative new start for the church; rather, the road to the future runs through the past.

These three matters—roots, connection, and authenticity in a changing world—will help us to maintain continuity with historic Christianity as the church moves forward. I hope what I cull from the past and then translate and adapt into the present will be beneficial to your ministry in the new cultural situation of our time.

Introduction

A Personal Note

I really started writing *Ancient-Future Worship* back in the seventies, not a few months ago. It was then that I began considering worship as a serious academic study. But, of course, I could not have written then what I have written today almost forty years later. I had to go through personal experiences and academic steps that have matured my reflection. (I write about these steps in the conclusion, "My Journey toward an Ancient-Future Worship.") In this book, probably my final book on worship, I invite you into that long worship journey.

This is not an academic book. I am less reliant on secondary sources and what other people think than I have been in my other worship books. However, this work is grounded in common worship studies that I have pondered for years and made my own. This reflection includes thinking that has accumulated and jelled over the past ten years. Consequently, it integrates Scripture, history, theology, culture, and missiology. Yet, *Ancient-Future Worship* is no rehash of material I have written in the past. It draws on recent studies in the Old Testament—especially Torah worship—and emphasizes the narrative nature of both the Bible and a worship that *does* God's story.

The Narrative Nature of Worship

What makes *Ancient-Future Worship* different from any other book I have written on worship is the central theme of recovering God's narrative. There are very pressing reasons why we should proclaim God's narrative in worship. The first, which is the main conviction of this book, is that God's narrative is the *truth*. The second reason to emphasize the narrative nature of worship is the current competition coming from terrorists who think that Allah narrates the world.

My wife and I are very interested in our world political situation. She spends more time at it than I do. She draws articles from the Internet, reads the *Wall Street Journal* and a number of political magazines, and listens to talk shows—and then distills the information for me.

Like most Americans we are deeply troubled by the Islamic terrorists and by what is happening in the Middle East. We love and support the Jewish nation, hope that Palestine can become an independent nation, and watch the craziness going on in Iran, Syria, Jordan, Saudi Arabia, Egypt, Lebanon, and, of course, the whole set of nations that comprise the Arab states.

While my wife is the expert in the political realm, we have also become interested in the history and theology of Islam. I am no expert, but I follow Muslim religious claims and have read a few books and parts of the Qur'an.

What should be of interest and concern to all Christians is the claim of radical Islam that Allah is the Lord of the universe and that he calls for the establishment of his domain over all the earth through the violent use of the sword. Allah, according to the Qur'an, is the one and only true and real God, who has revealed himself throughout history to many prophets including Moses, David, and Jesus. But his ultimate and authoritative revelation is to Muhammed, the final prophet. In order to fulfill Allah's narrative, radical Muslims are committed to destroy Western civilization, kill all the infidels, and bring the whole world under Allah and Sharia law (the way of life).

That is the radical Islam narrative—a story, a way of seeing and living in this world. It stands alongside and in competition with other narratives such as the secular narrative, the communist narrative, or any fascist narrative. Considering our world situation in this postmodern time, waiting, so to speak, for a fresh narrative to explain and pull together the world, why do we Christians stay focused on the modern world that privileges reason, science, consumerism, and marketing?

It is time to recover the truth—God's story of the world. And it is time to allow God's truthful story to shape our worship. The recovery of God's full and complete narrative from creation to re-creation is what makes *Ancient-Future Worship* unique among my worship books. Yes, you will find the story in my other books, but here, the development of that story in worship receives full attention.

How to Read This Book

Ancient-Future Worship is organized into two interconnected parts. In part 1, I present a brief description of worship as the story of God. In part 2, I apply the story of God to several, but not all, acts of worship.

I begin in chapter 1, "Worship *Does* God's Story," by getting back into the story of God as the place to start. I say "getting back into the story of God" because a dominant error of some Christians is to say, "I must bring God into *my* story." The ancient understanding is that God joins the story of humanity to *take us into his story.* There is a world of difference. One is narcissistic; the other is God-oriented. It will change your entire spiritual life when you realize that your life is joined to God's story. In worship we *remember* God's story in the past and *anticipate* God's story in the future.

In chapter 2, "Worship *Remembers* the Past," I focus on worship *remembering* God's story from the beginning to the present. This chapter emphasizes the place of creation, Israel, the incarnation, death, and resurrection.

Chapter 3, "Worship *Anticipates* the Future," is a call to hope in God's eternal reign over all creation. We often hope in ourselves, in our own planning for the future, in our vocation, and in our network of friends. But worship faithful to God's story says, "You're not in charge." Worship proclaims, "There is a connection between

God's past saving events and the future of the world." Worship that proclaims God's intended purpose for the world is saying, "Trust God. God has the best interests of the world and of you in mind. Evil is not the last word. God gets to say the last word. His vision drives our work and worship. It is a vision that will be completed at his second coming. He is Lord, not Allah—and the world will hear that message when we proclaim it in worship!"

This kind of worship will revolutionize our corporate worship and spirituality. However, as I wrote this book I asked, "Where do you find this kind of worship today?" This question drove my mind back into the longer history of the church, to moments in time when God's narrative was clearly the subject of worship. I found those places and times; however, the search made me painfully aware when God's narrative was not the subject of worship. Therefore, I wrote chapter 4, "How the *Fullness* of God's Story Became Lost." (Note that I use the word *fullness* because there are always at least vestiges of the story, even in the worst of times.)

In part 2, "Applying God's Story to Worship," I present how a worship that does God's story will effect congregational spirituality. I did not connect worship and spirituality when I first began to write about worship because I had not yet made the connection myself. The connection between worship and spirituality is made in God's story. Public worship *does* or *acts out* God's story. *Worship* is a verb. *Spirituality* is the contemplation of God's mighty saving deeds. Spirituality is, you might say, reflective. Yet worship does have a reflective side and spirituality has an active side. So the comparison is not absolute; it has some wiggle room. However, in both worship and spirituality we join God's story and find ourselves and the whole world under God's narrative. Neither worship nor spirituality has a life outside of God's narrative. God brings us into his story, his grace, his redeeming work in all of history. He does that in our worship. He does that in our spirituality.

In order for us to be brought into God's story, our worship needs to make a paradigm shift from self to God. I show how that can take place in chapter 5, "Worship: Transformed by Remembrance and Anticipation." In this chapter I simply apply these two biblical themes to our worship today and urge a recovery of remembrance and anticipation to the service of the Word, where the work of God in history is told, and to the service of the Eucharist, where God's story is both told and enacted or dramatized.

Next, I move on to look at the Word in more depth. I take up this theme in chapter 6, "Word: Transformed by the Narrative Nature of Scripture." Here I call us away from the rigid, dry, factual investigation and preaching of Scripture to the ancient way of reading the Bible as a whole through the recovery of biblical typology. Those who recover this ancient way of preaching will find new insights in the text, a new delight in preaching, and an overwhelming interest from the people who will learn a new love for the Word of God as they see remembrance and anticipation in the numerous types that draw the two Testaments together.

Then, I turn to communion in chapter 7, "Eucharist: Transformed by the Presence of God at Table." I deal with the absence of God at Table and the neglect with which the Table has been treated. It is a travesty that we have ignored Jesus's own words inviting us to meet him at the Table. He calls us there to remember him. But we have forgotten and wonder where he is. He calls us there to anticipate his kingdom rule over all creation, but we wonder what we have just done. And, looking for the meaning of the Eucharist within ourselves, we find nothing but disappointment; so we turn away.

Finally, I open a window to the ancient style of worship in chapter 8, "Prayer: Transformed by Recovering the Style of Ancient Worship." I am concerned over how worship has become a program, a show, and entertainment. Once again the problem is a self-centered and presentational approach to worship. If we think worship is about *me*, or if we are trying to *sell* people on worship and lure them to receive Jesus into their lives, then I can see the value of all entertaining programs. But once again, presentational worship turns true worship on its head. If worship is truly doing God's story and calling people to find their life and story by entering God's story, then the style of worship is prayer. I give an example of prayer worship from a fourth-century liturgy and invite you to take the time to actually pray sections of the service. As you do this you will experience the ancient way of worship and learn how to lead your people in worship-prayer.

In the conclusion I have made suggestions on what to read to help you make the paradigm shift toward an ancient-future worship. I am passionate about ancient-future worship; I believe it is the window of the church to the narrative of God.

We live in the most tumultuous time in my memory, and I am in my seventh decade of life. There appears to be a gathering storm in the Middle East; the influence of Christian faith seems to be so individualized that it no longer makes an impact on culture. What is decent, upright, honest, and God-respecting seems to be falling all around us, replaced with crudity and a freedom that goes beyond the bounds of respect for those who wish to live disciplined and passionate lives. Where can we start in this crazy world to set up a beacon of light, a standard of truth, a path toward God's will? I recognize there are many ministries doing just that. But, I find one key ministry lacking—worship. And this book is all about how to restore a worship that will once again show the way—the narrative of God, the only true narrative of the world!

I strongly urge you to read the conclusion, "My Journey toward an Ancient-Future Worship" *before you read the body of the text.*

Part 1

Rediscovering God's Story in Worship

1

Worship *Does* God's Story

*S*ome time ago a pastor friend of mine looked me in the eye and asked, "What is worship? Give me a one-liner that will solve my confusion." I shot back the four words of this chapter title: "Worship does God's story!"

The pastor's face froze. He looked back at me with his head moving side to side in a "What's that mean?" motion. "Bob," he said, "I haven't the slightest idea what you are talking about. Tell me, what does it mean to say that worship does God's story?"

I have written *Ancient-Future Worship* to answer that question.

Where do you begin? Obviously, we have the whole Bible before us, the entire history of the church, and our contemporary situation to consider. I could start anywhere—with Genesis, the Exodus event, the Christ event, the ancient church, or even the contemporary situation. However, I am going to start with the description of Pentecost—Acts 2—and you will see why.

The Pentecost Proclamation

The day of Pentecost is certainly a turning point in history. It is a day of ending, but it also is a day of beginning.

We generally associate Pentecost with the coming of the Holy Spirit, as if the Spirit originated on that day. Yet actually, the Holy Spirit has been present in all of history. The story of God is the story of the Triune God, and therefore always the story of God the Father, God the Son, and God the Holy Spirit. For example, an image used by the early church fathers was that God always works in the world through his own two hands—the incarnate Word and the Holy Spirit.

So the Spirit is at work, as is the Son, together with the Father in creation, in the Exodus event, and in the history and symbols of Israel. In Scripture we meet the Holy Spirit in creation "hovering over the waters" (Gen. 1:2) and in the inspiration of the prophets delivering the Word of God. The Holy Spirit speaks judgment in the coming forth of John the Baptist, effects the incarnation in the birth of Jesus, affirms the ministry of Jesus in his baptism, and is active in redemption through his ministry, death, resurrection, and ascension.

On the day of Pentecost, ten days after the ascension, we see the work of the Holy Spirit again. Just as the Spirit is at work in creation and the incarnation, now the Holy Spirit is at work in re-creation, the redemption and restoration of the creation, announced by the Spirit on the day of Pentecost. So then, if the Holy Spirit has been present in all God's redemptive action, what is the *new* work that the Holy Spirit is doing on the day of Pentecost?

What is new is not the *coming* of the Holy Spirit, for the Holy Spirit, described by the Nicene Creed (AD 325) is "the Lord, the giver of life," the very source and energy of creation. Wherever there is life, it is always the work of the Spirit. What then is *new*?

Two words capture what is new. New *understanding* and new *empowerment*. The new understanding is summarized by Peter's sermon on Pentecost Sunday. The people, amazed at the message of God delivered in their own tongue, ask, "What does this mean?" (Acts 2:12). Then Peter stands up and speaks (Acts 2:14–36). Drawing from the *history of Israel* and the *events of the crucifixion*, he concludes, "God has made this Jesus whom you crucified to be both Lord and Messiah" (Acts 2:36 NLT). The Triune God, who had been active in history, has brought the world to this moment. The *new* understanding is that the long-expected Messiah has come, that this Messiah is Lord of all creation, and that people are to repent, be baptized for the forgiveness of their sins, and receive the Holy Spirit. Human history has reached a turning point in the coming of the Messiah, the Lord of all creation. The story of God working in history has come to a climactic point at Pentecost, and now God's narrative, which seemed confined to Israel, is to be known by all for all. God's narrative is the story of all creatures and creation. He will renew the earth!

There are many ways to summarize and present this great story that has come together in Jesus Christ and has been announced at Pentecost. The Bible is full of images, word pictures, stories, types, and analogies that proclaim the story. One way to tell this story is through four pictures: God and the Garden of Eden; God and the desert; God and the Garden of Gethsemane; God and the eternal garden.

In the modern world we seldom looked at the Bible as a composite picture revealing a cosmic vision of the world; we were too busy with the details to see God's narrative whole. We were too concerned with analyzing its parts, with literary criticism, historical verification, and theological systems. However, the mood now has shifted to the broad strokes. So I turn now to the four pictures that tie it all together—at the risk of not dealing with the details that continue to interest many. So read it for the picture—get a vision of the whole.

God and the Garden of Eden

God's story starts with God himself. The biblical God is no monad, no impersonal force, but a Triune community of Father, Son, and Holy Spirit. The emphasis falls on community. God is one. Christians do not embrace polytheism as Muslims charge.

This Triune community is a person and is personal. The biblical and ancient definition of *person* is "a being in community." God is an eternal community of love. If God was a monad, God would be neither personal nor communal.

God, this eternal being of love, desires to create other beings (persons in community) to share in his own community. God creates

31

humanity in his *image*, persons who dwell in community and are actually called by God to fellowship with the community of the Godhead from the *inside*.

He first creates a world—a *place* of habitation for himself, a place for other beings made in his image to dwell in communion with himself. The Garden of Eden is this place. It is the place of God's creativity, the place of God's habitation. The idyllic description of the garden in Genesis is a picture of how God wants his world to be and how God and humanity commune.

The picture is one of relationship. Adam and Eve in harmony with God, with each other, and with nature.

The picture is also one of work—humanity caring for the earth—naming the animals, finding purpose in doing God's will of cultivating the earth, unfolding its treasures, continually making the earth the habitation of God's glory, the theater of his praise.

God and the Desert

The second biblical picture is God and the desert. The fall has corrupted the relationships of the Garden of Eden. Now the communion between God and humanity, humanity with neighbor, and humanity with God is disrupted, broken, torn, and twisted. Evil has entered the picture.

Evil is not a mere absence of good or moral failure. Evil is a human refusal to carry out God's purposes. Evil is a deliberate, intentional, and violent rejection of God. It is a choice to unfold culture away from God. It is life and work in the service of Satan—the anti-God—the father of all that is sin and death in the world.

Evil results in death: "Therefore, just as sin entered the world through one man, *and death through sin*, and in this way death came to all men, because all sinned" (Rom. 5:12, emphasis added).

Death now reigns in creation.

Death is that dark tide of evil that envelops all creation, all creatures, all culture making, all cities, and all civilization.

Death paralyzes humanity and brings closure to all life.

Death touches every tree, every blade of grass, and every flower, and it turns God's garden into a desert.

The desert is the archetypical symbol of the world hostile to God. It is the symbol of all that is antilife, the symbol of the dead earth the wind blows dry. The sun's heat dries up the world, the ground becomes parched and dry, and the ground itself cries out under the burden of its own death. The desert has become Sartre's *No Exit*, T. S. Eliot's *The Waste Land*, Samuel Beckett's *Waiting for Godot*.

Yet in the desert God raises up a witness to the garden lost and the garden yet to come. He forms for himself a family in Abraham, a tribe in Jacob, a nation in Israel, a kingdom in David. In this family, in this people whom God calls to himself, there is a root—the root of Jesse, a branch in the desert with a blossom, a blossom of life, of hope, of newness—a promise that through Abraham's family:

> I will make you into a great nation
> > and I will bless you;
> I will make your name great,
> > and you will be a blessing.
> I will bless those who bless you,
> > and whoever curses you I will curse;
> and all peoples on earth
> > will be blessed through you.

Genesis 12:2–3

Here we find, in the words given to Abraham, the promise of redemption, the rescue of the whole world.

The nation of Israel is a direct result of God's promise. Out of this nation God's anointed one will come—God's Messiah who is Lord of all creation.

Israel is full of signs, types, and figures of the one to come: Israel is now in the desert under the hard hand of Pharaoh. Their bondage is the symbol of all creatures burdened by the alienation of the desert. Moses is the archetypical symbol of Jesus, the leader sent by God to deliver his people from their bondage in the desert (Heb. 3:1–6). The mighty hand of God in the Exodus event by whose power Israel is delivered from their bondage is a type of the Christ event—the incarnation, crucifixion, and resurrection—through which all creatures and creation are redeemed and restored to the wholeness of the garden (Heb. 2:5–18).

33

The forming of Israel into a people is a type of the church—the people of God called to be God's community, to enter into communion with him as in the garden (1 Peter 2:9–10). Everything within Israel is ultimately about the Messiah to come (Luke 24:27).

The tabernacle was the place of God's presence even as God dwelt in his incarnate Word (John 1:14). The tabernacle also foreshadowed all the work of Jesus—the new covenant he brings for eternal life, his high priestly ministry, the eternal worship, and salvation through his shed blood (Hebrews 7–10).

The desert of hostility against God with all of its symbols of death is not so barren that there is no sign of hope. That hope is found in Israel, from whom the Messiah will come. He is the one who will reverse the effects of the fall and restore the desert once again into the garden of God's glory.

God and the Garden of Gethsemane

The Garden of Gethsemane is the garden of reversal. It is new water for the parched ground. It is new blood for the life of the world. For here the new creation begins. The sin of the first-formed man is amended by the second Adam. "For just as through the disobedience of the one man the many were made sinners, so also through the obedience of the one man the many will be made righteous" (Rom. 5:19).

I was flying from San Francisco to Los Angeles when I entered into a conversation with a man of Eastern descent on the subject of faith. "Tell me," I asked, "What is a good one-liner that captures the essence of your faith?"

"Sure," he said and quickly responded with these words: "We are all part of the problem. We are all part of the solution."

"Would you like to hear a Christian one-liner?" I asked.

"Well, yes, of course," he answered.

"We are all part of the problem," I said, pausing long enough for the connection to be made. "But," I added, "there is only one man who is the solution. His name is Jesus."

Paul, in his letter to the Corinthians, catches this one-liner in these words: "Since death came through a man, the resurrection of the dead comes also through a man. For as in Adam all die, so in Christ all will be made alive" (1 Cor. 15:21–22).

This second Adam who redeems creature and creation and restores God's garden at the end of history is God himself, the incarnate Word. No human being can restore the garden. Only God can do that, and he does it by becoming one of us, taking on the curse of sin itself—death. By dying for us he destroys death and is raised to new life. His resurrection is a second act of creation, a new beginning that will be culminated in his coming again to reestablish the garden, to bring humanity into his own communal life, and to rule over creation forever.

The Incarnation

A key to God's work in Jesus Christ to renew and restore all creatures and creation is the incarnation. In the incarnation, God unites with our humanity in Jesus Christ. The profound meaning of this incarnate union is often missed by those who glibly affirm the union of God and man in Jesus Christ but don't reflect on its meaning.

The early church fathers reflect deeply on the incarnation and how it is connected to creation and the fall and on its intrinsic relationship to the cross, the empty tomb, the ascension, the eternal intercession of Christ, and his second coming to restore the garden in the new heavens and new earth.

Reflection on the incarnation and its connection to every aspect of God's story is the missing link in today's theological reflection and worship. The link is found in these words: *God does for us what we cannot do for ourselves.*

Consider this: God places humanity in the garden to enjoy intimate relationship with God inside the community of Father, Son, and Holy Spirit. God invites us to share in his own life and to participate with him to make his creation a place of his glory. We fail. We spurn God. We unfold the world, its culture, and civilization after the will of anti-God, Satan. We now can have no part of God. Because of our sin and wickedness, we are unable through any effort of our own to enter, ever again, into the intimacy of the community enjoyed by the Father, Son, and Holy Spirit.

35

So God himself, the incarnate Word, takes up residence (unites) with our fallen self so that he, God, now as a man, can reverse the human condition. He lifts, so to speak, all our sin and rebellion into himself. He lives the perfect life—the life God wanted for us in obedience to his created purpose—and reverses the life of fallen humanity. He pays the penalty for sin on the cross. He defeats the devil. He conquers hell. He re-creates. He does all this so that when we trust in him, he is in us and we in him. Once again, because of his incarnation followed by his death and resurrection, we in him are restored and now enter into the intimate communion and fellowship of the community of Father, Son, and Spirit. And this is all because God, out of his great love and mercy, became incarnate, united with the human race, and reversed the human situation.

Creation and Redemption

The incarnation brings creation and redemption together. This emphasis is unique among all the religions of the world. For example, the Hebrews affirm God as Creator but have no one to redeem the creation (although the typologies fulfilled in Christ are numerous). Then there are the Muslims. Allah is Creator, but again, there is not redemption of creation. Islam is a religion of law. The Creator has given to the world the rules we are to live by. They are found in Sharia law, and those who do not follow the rules are punished in violent ways.

How does creation get redeemed in most religions? It doesn't. Redemption, instead, is escape from the world. Through religious techniques of meditation, prayer, chanting, and the like, the soul can momentarily escape its bodily material existence and unite temporarily with transcendence. However, the self must return to its prison until the final relief in death.

The New Agers are trying to change Christianity to follow this direction. In New Age books and literature, Jesus is now treated as a guru whose main purpose was to show people how to transcend their earthbound selves and get in touch with the transcendent spirit.

For this reason, among others, it is imperative for us to recover the narrative of the creator God who becomes involved in our creation to redeem it. Christians have this conviction in their spiritual DNA, but I think it has been neglected, perhaps even ignored, in the last fifty years.

I find, for example, that liberal Christians have a creation theology without an incarnation. Consequently, liberal Christianity ends up being a humanitarian social action (as opposed to a redemptive social witness).

I find a similar kind of problem among conservative Christians. Conservatives have a redemption theology. But they focus almost entirely on the death of Jesus and therefore ignore the connection between creation, incarnation, and re-creation. Consequently, conservative Christianity concentrates on snatching the soul from the body to save it from hell. This kind of Christianity is another kind of separation of creation and redemption that leans toward Gnosticism, an early Christian heresy that opposed belief in the incarnation and redemption of the whole world.

The Union of the Divine and Human

The incarnation of God is the Word made flesh (John 1:14). God literally and actually became a human being. God did not *turn into* flesh, nor did the Word simply *reside* in a human body. The incarnation is a real *union* of divinity and humanity that took place in the womb of the Virgin Mary. This perfect union is described by the Chalcedon Creed (AD 451) as one that took place

> without confusion, without change, without division, without separation; the distinction of natures being in no way annulled by the union, but rather the characteristics of each nature being preserved and coming together to form one person and substance, not as parted or separated into two persons, but one and the same Son and only-begotten God the Word, Lord Jesus Christ; even as the prophets from earliest times spoke of him, and our Lord Jesus Christ himself taught us, and the creed of the fathers handed down to us.[1]

We popularize this union when we refer to Jesus as 100 percent divine and 100 percent human. This is certainly a good and accurate description, but we need to plumb its depth.

Take time to reflect on the divine presence of God in the human person Jesus. There is never a separation of the divine from the human. The divine presence is at work in the gestation of Jesus in the womb of Mary, in the young life of Jesus, his maturation, his baptism, his sermons, his miracles. The divine presence is discounted by those who reject God's presence in the events surrounding the crucifixion, death and burial, resurrection and ascension, and now his eternal intercession for us, and soon, his return to restore the world to its pristine state.

Then, too, the human presence is always there united to the divine in the entirety of his incarnation. In the human presence all of humanity has been united to God. Jesus took to himself, received into himself, assumed into himself (there really are no words that fully describe the mystery of this union), the entirety of human rebellion and the death that hangs over every creature and all creation.

Because of the union of the divine and human, God, in Jesus, by the power of the Spirit, perfectly recapitulates the first Adam. *Recapitulation* is a word that conveys the meaning of a Greek word used in Ephesians 1:9–10: "He made known to us the mystery of his will according to his good pleasure, which he purposed in Christ, to be put into effect when the times have reached their fulfillment—to bring all things in heaven and earth together [recapitulate] under one head, even Christ." This *recapitulation* of all things is accomplished by God in order to begin the creation again and bring it to its perfection in the everlasting garden.

What happened in the Garden of Gethsemane is the turning point of God's relationship to the world. This turning point was witnessed to in Israel. It began to be on display physically in the incarnation. In the womb of Mary, Christ was already in full obedience to the Father, where he began the process of forming the new man. The life, crucifixion, death, descent into hell, resurrection, and ascension fulfilled the hope of Israel for a world Redeemer. Jesus, the Messiah, is now resurrected and ascended as Lord over all the powers and principalities. By his sacrifice for sin, he has won a great victory over all that is evil and death (promised in Gen. 3:15). Jesus Christ has "disarmed the powers and authorities,

38

he made a public spectacle of them, triumphing over them by the cross" (Col. 2:15).

God's Eternal Garden

We now live in that period of history between the resurrection and the second coming of Christ. When he comes again he will restore his world and remake the garden.

God will dwell in that garden as the place of his eternal habitation and glory. And the creatures he made for communion with his Triune community of love will share (through their union with his incarnate Son and Holy Spirit) an eternal communion with the Triune God. Then, in this new eternal state, his will shall be done "on earth as it is in heaven" (Matt. 6:10).

Back to Peter's sermon on the day of Pentecost: The final words of his sermon (Acts 2:36) speak directly to the picture of the lordship of Jesus Christ over all things. The Messiah of Israel, the one longed for and hoped for, the Redeemer of the whole world, has come. The next chapter of human history, which began on Pentecost, is to proclaim God's redeeming presence in Jesus Christ and to proclaim the hope for the world that is coming. Jesus is Lord. Some day the whole world will bow the knee and confess him to be the Lord of all creation (Phil. 2:10–11).

In the meantime, Acts 2:38 describes the expected response to God's narrative of the world. It is to "repent and be baptized, every one of you, in the name of Jesus Christ for the forgiveness of your sins. And you will receive the gift of the Holy Spirit."

The same Spirit that brought forth life from the waters of the earth, from the Red Sea, and from the Jordan, brings us the new birth. We are baptized into Jesus Christ. We now have a new identity. We are members of the body of Christ, the church.

The church is all about the continuation of God's narrative in this world. Now, finally, worship. What does it mean to say, "Worship does God's story?" It is this: *Worship proclaims, enacts, and sings God's story*. Worship is not a program. Nor is worship about *me*. Worship is a narrative—God's narrative of the world from its

39

beginning to its end. How will the world know its own story unless we do that story in public worship?

Conclusion

I began this chapter with the story of my pastor friend who had no idea what I was talking about when I said that "worship does God's story." In a world where worship follows the culture and becomes like another TV program—presenting, entertaining, satisfying to religious consumerism—it is no wonder that even a pastor trained in seminary knows little to nothing about the meaning of worship.

The problem goes even deeper, however. It goes to the heart of the Good News. Worship—daily, weekly, yearly—is rooted in the gospel. And when worship fails to proclaim, sing, and enact at the Table the Good News that God not only saves sinners but also narrates the whole world, it is not only worship that becomes corrupted by the culture, it is also the gospel. Not only has worship lost its way, but the fullness of the gospel, the story which worship does, has been lost.

So this book is not only about recovering worship, it is also about recovering God's Good News for the whole world. Once we have recovered God's Good News, the great and incredible news that he is the one who by his own two hands—the incarnate Word and the Holy Spirit—has recovered the garden, then, knowing this cosmic content, we can enter into the fullness of worship again. Worship gathers to sing, tell, and enact God's story of the world from its beginning to its end. Glory be to God who is Creator and Redeemer of all that is!

2

Worship *Remembers* the Past

*T*ake yourself back to your high school or college days for a few moments. Remember your curriculum. If your class schedule was like mine, it suffered from a terrible fragmentation. All day long I, and I am sure you, attended classes that were never integrated with each other. One class is on history, another on math, then chemistry, followed by language. It seems as though curriculum planners never sat down and asked, "How can we unfold our curriculum in such a way that our students will see things whole?"

I refer to this example because we have all experienced it. Fragmentation not only permeates education, it appears to be a part of life in general. And, unfortunately, it plagues the church and especially its worship.

The Fragmentation of Worship

Fragmentation in worship is expressed in a worship that emphasizes one or another aspect of God's story but neglects the story as a whole. For example, some Christian fellowships concentrate on only one person of the Trinity.

If God is worshiped only as Father, he is seen as Creator—the giver of the gift of beauty in creation—or as Love—the source of all that is good in the world. Or God is the benevolent Father who cares for the poor and marginalized. Sermons, hymns, songs, prayers, and communion will emphasize these themes, calling on us to care for creation, love our neighbor, and care for the poor.

These themes—creation, love, justice, and mercy—are of course biblical themes and are to be emphasized in our worship. Without the supernatural themes of incarnation, redemption, and eschatological re-creation, however, these themes of creation, love of neighbor, and justice for all lose their distinct Christian content and have little more power than humanistic values of ecology, love of neighbor, and care for the poor.

Then there are those Christian groups who concentrate on the work of the Son—God is to be worshiped as the Redeemer. The emphasis falls on the death of the Son. He is the sacrifice for our sins. He took our place and died for us to satisfy the justice of God. We stand in the righteousness of Christ. God sees us through the work of Christ so that we are forgiven sinners, gaining eternal life through Jesus Christ. Of course these themes are all biblical. However, when these themes are presented without creation and without God's incarnation into our creation to re-create it, God's whole story is reduced to individualism. God saves this or that individual, but he does not save and restore the whole world. In these fellowships the songs and choruses are usually *me*-centered, the preaching is often based on therapeutic themes, and communion is a sober reflection on the death of Jesus without any reference to his resurrection, exaltation, and sure return to claim his lordship over all creatures and creation.

Then there are those fellowships that are centered on the Spirit. The emphasis falls on being open to the Spirit, receiving the gift of tongues, and ministries of healing. Obviously these are all biblical themes and should not be disregarded. These communities don't disregard the work of the Son, but they often have a reduced, individualistic view of God's work similar to those fellowships described above. In addition, their strong emphasis on the work of the Spirit in each individual life elevates personal experience, not only above the cosmic story of God, but in some cases to the exclusion of God's story for the whole world. When creation, incarnation, and re-creation of the whole world are replaced by the experience of the Spirit, the believer becomes preoccupied with his or her own story.

The issue that all of us need to deal with is the reduction and fragmentation of God's *whole* story. The full story is that of the work of the Father, the Son, and the Holy Spirit. God creates, becomes involved with creation, and is made incarnate into time, space, and history in order to redeem and restore the world as the garden of God's habitation and people as his community of love and fellowship.

In summary, here is what biblical worship does: It remembers God's work in the past, anticipates God's rule over all creation, and actualizes both past and future in the present to transform persons, communities, and the world.

Biblical Worship *Remembers* God's Saving Deeds

Remembering is the opposite of forgetting. When we forget the past, the past is dead in our lives. Humanly speaking, most of us take a certain delight in remembering our lives, our families, and our heritage. Some of us spend numerous hours searching out our ancestry, making lines of descent, and putting them in scrapbooks for our children.

Biblical remembering is much more than an intellectual recalling. Biblical remembering brings God's saving events to mind, body, and soul. Biblical remembering makes the power and the saving effect of the event present to the worshiping community. When we take bread and wine, for example, Jesus Christ, by the power of the Spirit, is made accessible through the faith of those who see him and his saving work through the symbols of his broken body and shed blood. The word *remembrance* (in Greek, *anamnēsis*) has the force of "making present," "making alive," "making real." Remembrance is also directed to God. It says, "God, remember your saving deeds—remember how you delivered us from the power of the evil one and conquered death."

It may seem strange to say worship reminds God, but think of it— the content of God's saving deeds is the content of eternal heavenly worship. God loves his own story. God's story is to his glory, why

we want to return to remembering ourselves

wouldn't he love it? So, God loves our worship when we remember his saving deeds in Jesus Christ. Our worship tells that old, old story. That's the story God gave the world, and that story is the content of worship. Through worship the world learns its own story. And how will others hear unless we do God's story in worship, calling people to remember God's story?

I live among Swedes in a place called Bethany Beach on the shores of Lake Michigan. This place was founded by Baptist and Evangelical Covenant Swedes in 1906. This year, as I write this book, they celebrated their hundred-year anniversary. A ten-day festival was filled with speeches, activities, films, pictures, and icons of the past. In a community of about four hundred people, more than a thousand came who had been touched by life and ministry at Bethany Beach because they wanted to remember. The remembrance was a huge emotional and spiritual awakening as we all gathered around the theme: "100 years of God's faithfulness." A few people had forgotten but were awakened by the recovery of memory. Some, like myself, a non-Swede and a more recent arrival in this community of faith, learned the memory and became inspired by the way God has visited this place and raised up a witness to himself far beyond the few acres we occupy in southern Michigan.

So it is with worship. Forgetting brings death, but remembering brings life.

Worship Is Situated in the Story It Remembers

Biblical and ancient worship is never about *me and my worship.* Instead, biblical and ancient worship is always about *remembering all of God's saving acts in history.* (Obviously worship has to do with my faith response to God's saving actions in history.)

One Old Testament passage that clearly enunciates the remembering pattern of worship is found in Deuteronomy 6. Here God instructs Moses on how to remember. God himself knows the dead end of forgetting, so he tells Moses:

In the future, when your son asks you, "What is the meaning of the stipulations, decrees and laws the LORD our God has commanded you?" tell him: "We were slaves of Pharaoh in Egypt, but the LORD

44

brought us out of Egypt with a mighty hand. Before our eyes the
LORD sent miraculous signs and wonders—great and terrible—upon
Egypt and Pharaoh and his whole household. But he brought us out
from there to bring us in and give us the land that he promised on
oath to our forefathers. The LORD commanded us to obey all these
decrees and to fear the LORD our God, so that we might always
prosper and be kept alive, as is the case today. And if we are careful
to obey all this law before the LORD our God, as he has commanded
us, that will be our righteousness."

Deuteronomy 6:20–25

In this admonition we see that not only worship is situated in memory, but also spirituality and ethics are grounded in the memory
that elicits a right faith and an obedient life.

This same theme—the integration of worship, spirituality, and
ethics—is brought together in the compelling passage of Peter written to the Christians under persecution by Nero and subject to
forgetting. Peter tells them:

You are a chosen people, a royal priesthood, a holy nation, a people
belonging to God, *that you may declare the praises of him who called
you out of darkness into his wonderful light.* Once you were not a
people, but now you are the people of God; once you had not received
mercy, but now you have received mercy.

Dear friends, I urge you, as aliens and strangers in the world, to
abstain from sinful desires, which war against your soul. Live such
good lives among the pagans that, though they accuse you of doing
wrong, they may see your good deeds and glorify God on the day
he visits us.

1 Peter 2:9–12, emphasis added

Peter, as in the Old Testament passage cited above, brings memory
together with worship, spirituality, and ethics. When we remember God's mighty, saving deeds, we are inspired to worship him,
to contemplate his mighty deeds, and to obey him. Remembering
is that powerful!

Pick up your favorite concordance—Strong's or Young's or one
that is more simple—and look up the word *remember.* There you
will find what it is that biblical people do at worship; they remember

God's saving acts in history. And if you read on you will find, bound together with this remembering, instructions on spirituality and ethics. Consider these few pertinent passages from Deuteronomy:

- Remember how God appeared before you in his awesome presence at Mt. Horeb (4:10).
- Remember how God redeemed you from slavery in Egypt (5:15; 15:15; 16:12; 24:18; 24:22).
- Remember the power by which he humbled Pharaoh (7:18).
- Remember how God provided for you as he led you through the desert for forty years (8:2).
- Remember how God gives you the ability to produce wealth as he swore to your forefathers (8:18).
- Remember how God gives you the land because of who he is, not because of what you have done (9:7).
- Remember God showed you his mighty deeds, before your very eyes (11:2–7).
- Remember the haste and affliction of your God's Passover (16:3).
- Remember God's power to both afflict and heal, as he did with Miriam (24:9).
- Remember the days of old (32:7).

In the New Testament God is presented as the one who does not forget. The entire Song of Mary, the Magnificat, is a praise of the God who remembers his own promises. Prayerfully reflect on this glorious passage of Scripture that opens to us the activity of God, which we also are to remember. Throughout history Mary's song has been sung in worship as found in every prayer book text:

> My soul glorifies the Lord
>   and my spirit rejoices in God my Savior,
> for he has been mindful
>   of the humble state of his servant.
> From now on all generations will call me blessed,
>   for the Mighty One has done great things for me—
> holy is his name.

46

His mercy extends to those who fear him,
>from generation to generation.
He has performed mighty deeds with his arm;
>he has scattered those who are proud in their inmost
>thoughts.
He has brought down rulers from their thrones
>but has lifted up the humble.
He has filled the hungry with good things
>but has sent the rich away empty.
He has helped his servant Israel,
>remembering to be merciful
to Abraham and his descendants forever,
>even as he said to our fathers.

Luke 1:46–55

Look at the five early Christian sermons in the book of Acts— every one of them is based on the memory of how God has acted in history and has now acted in Jesus Christ to rescue the world from sin and death (see Acts 2:14–36; 3:12–26; 4:8–12; 5:29–32; 7:2–53). I will quote the shortest of these sermons to show the heart of biblical preaching—the Good News. The sermons all emphasize how we are to remember that the former times have been fulfilled in Jesus Christ, that a new era has come, and that we are called to repent and submit to Jesus as Lord.

Peter and the other apostles replied: "We must obey God rather than men! The God of our fathers raised Jesus from the dead—whom you had killed by hanging him on a tree. God exalted him to his own right hand as Prince and Savior that he might give repentance and forgiveness of sins to Israel. We are witnesses of these things, and so is the Holy Spirit, whom God has given to those who obey him."

Acts 5:29–32

Then consider the admonition of Jesus to his disciples in Matthew 26:26–29. He says that you, too, have a way of remembering him. Paul picks up on this theme of remembrance in his classic words on the Lord's Supper:

For I received from the Lord what I also passed on to you: The Lord Jesus, on the night he was betrayed, took bread, and when he had given thanks, he broke it and said, "This is my body, which is for you; do this in *remembrance* of me." In the same way, after supper he took the cup, saying, "This cup is the new covenant in my blood; do this, whenever you drink it, in *remembrance* of me." For whenever you eat this bread and drink this cup, you proclaim the Lord's death until he comes.

1 Corinthians 11:23–26, emphasis added

How Worship Remembers God's Saving Deeds

On the question of how worship remembers God's saving deeds, we find, once again, a remarkable unity between the worship of Israel and the worship of the church. In brief, the saving deeds of God are remembered through *historical recitation* and *dramatic reenactment.*

Remembering through Historical Recitation

In both Hebrew and Christian worship God's saving deeds are remembered in the historical recitation of preaching, creed, and song. Three examples are sufficient.

1. Preaching. One of the major ways to recite and thus remember God's actions in history on behalf of God's people is through preaching. The entire book of Deuteronomy is a sermon. The sermon that recounts God's mighty saving deeds for Israel ends with these striking words,

No prophet has risen in Israel like Moses, whom the LORD knew face to face, who did all those miraculous signs and wonders the LORD sent him to do in Egypt—to Pharaoh and to all his officials and to his whole land. For no one has ever shown the mighty power or performed the awesome deeds that Moses did in the sight of all Israel.

Deuteronomy 34:10–12

I have previously mentioned the five sermons in the book of Acts—all recitations of God's great deeds of salvation. Preaching,

48

throughout Scripture, is always about God and how he has entered into the history of the world to rescue and save it. There is a great need today to rediscover biblical preaching—the recitation of God's mighty acts of salvation.

2. Creeds. Both testaments also present creeds that are recited as part of worship. Since worship remembers God's saving action, creeds are sound-bite testimonies to God's long activity to bring about his purposes for the world. The most stunning Hebrew creed is found in Deuteronomy 26:5–9:

> My father was a wandering Aramean, and he went down into Egypt with a few people and lived there and became a great nation, powerful and numerous. But the Egyptians mistreated us and made us suffer, putting us to hard labor. Then we cried out to the LORD, the God of our fathers, and the LORD heard our voice and saw our misery, toil and oppression. So the LORD brought us out of Egypt with a mighty hand and an outstretched arm, with great terror and with miraculous signs and wonders. He brought us to this place and gave us this land, a land flowing with milk and honey.

This creed is recited by the worshipers during the firstfruits festival. The worshiper brings the basket of firstfruits to the priest, who then sets it before the altar. The creed is then said by the worshipers, followed by the words, "And now I bring the firstfruits of the soil that you, O LORD, have given me" (Deut. 26:10). These gifts are then distributed to the poor—demonstrating the relationship between worship as thanksgiving for God's goodness and worship as an extension of God's justice to the poor and needy.

Similar summaries of God's saving acts are found in the New Testament and are forerunners of the Apostles' Creed, which summarizes God's actions in history. One such New Testament passage is 1 Timothy 3:16:

> He appeared in a body,
>   was vindicated by the Spirit,
> was seen by angels,
>   was preached among the nations,
> was believed on in the world,
>   was taken up in glory.

3. Songs. The Bible is also full of songs that commemorate God's actions in history. If you have the time, take as a devotional challenge the reading and studying of the Psalms. Note how many of them recount God's saving action and praise God for the many ways he has intervened in history to save Israel and the world. One great Old Testament hymn known by nearly every Christian is the Song of Moses and Miriam to celebrate the great deliverance of Israel from the Egyptians displayed at the Red Sea. The song begins with these words:

> I will sing to the LORD,
>   for he is highly exalted.
> The horse and its rider
>   he has hurled into the sea.
>
> Exodus 15:1

After recounting God's deliverance the song ends:

> Sing to the LORD,
>   for he is highly exalted.
> The horse and its rider
>   he has hurled into the sea.
>
> Exodus 15:12

The New Testament also has its share of songs exalting the work of the Lord in history. The songs, known as "Christ-hymns," are particularly poignant with their emphasis on God's descent into our history to recover the world for himself and God's ascent in victory over his enemies to rule over the world. The best known of these hymns is found in Paul's letter to the Philippians 2:6–11. Take some time to delight in its message:

> Who, being in very nature God,
>   did not consider equality with God something to be
>   grasped,
> but made himself nothing,
>   taking the very nature of a servant,
>   being made in human likeness.
> And being found in appearance as a man,

> he humbled himself
> and became obedient to death—even death on a cross!
> Therefore God exalted him to the highest place
> and gave him the name that is above every name,
> that at the name of Jesus every knee should bow,
> in heaven and on earth and under the earth,
> and every tongue confess that Jesus Christ is Lord,
> to the glory of God the Father.

These examples from preaching, creed, and song are only a few of the many examples of remembering through historical worship. They should remind us that remembering is not a mere recounting of historical information, but a remembering that recalls the mystery of God at work in history saving a people and ultimately the world. This kind of remembering creates life and keeps God's community from forgetting—for to forget is a sure sign of death. As if historical recitation was not enough, God has given us another way to remember his mighty saving acts—*dramatic reenactment*.

Remembering through Dramatic Reenactment

Just as historical recitation is not the repetition of factual information, so also dramatic reenactment is not a mere empty symbol of a bygone historical event. Instead, dramatic reenactment draws the worshiper into the action, not as an observer, but as a participant. Both Hebrew and Christian worship focus on God's saving events enacted within the worshiping community. The most prominent examples of dramatic reenactment are found in the correspondences between the Hebrew sacrificial rituals and the Lord's Supper, the Hebrew Passover and the Great Paschal Vigil developed by the early Christian community, and the sacred cycle of the Hebrew year with the cycle of the Christian year.

First, let's look at how the *sacrificial rituals of Hebrew worship and the Lord's Supper* are dramatic reenactments of God's saving deeds. Space does not permit the development here of all the Old Testament sacrifices and rituals, but what they enact is an *approach* to God. These rituals are, as the writer of Hebrews states, "a shadow of the good things that are coming" (Heb. 10:1). That is, these rituals point to Christ, to the shedding of his blood for the life of the

51

world. In Old Testament worship the rituals of the shedding of blood were rituals based on the covenant between God and Israel (Exod. 24:1–8). These rituals sealed the covenant and made it clear that "without the shedding of blood there is no forgiveness" (Heb. 9:22). While all the sacrificial rituals point to the sacrifice of Christ for the sins of the world, none were more poignant than the rituals enacted on the Day of Atonement. On this day the high priest entered into the Holy of Holies and sacrificed a goat on behalf of the priesthood. In another ritual the high priest laid hands on a second goat, confessing over it the sins of the nation. This goat, the scapegoat, was sent into the uninhabited wilderness bearing the sins of the people. The first goat was sacrificed to symbolize the blood atonement for sin; the second goat was sent away to symbolize the removal of sin (Lev. 16:7–10).

Let's compare the enacting of Old Testament sacrifices with what we Christians do at the Table. The Lord's Supper is the worship ritual that reenacts Christ's sacrifice of himself for the sins of the world. It is the primary way of reenacting the sacrifice of Christ that fulfills all Hebrew sacrificial expectations. This reenactment of Christ's blood sacrifice comes to us with the force of tradition. By tradition, I mean to say, "It's crucial to do this." Paul claims to have received this mandate for frequent communion from the Lord himself.

> *For I received from the Lord what I also passed on to you:* The Lord Jesus on the night he was betrayed, took bread, and when he had given thanks, he broke it and said, "This is my body, which is for you; do this in remembrance of me." In the same way, after supper he took the cup, saying, "This cup is the new covenant in my blood; do this, whenever you drink it, in remembrance of me." For whenever you eat this bread and drink this cup, you proclaim the Lord's death until he comes.
>
> 1 Corinthians 11:23–26, emphasis added

Not all Christian groups are obedient to the communion mandate. For example, I spoke once to a group of ministers on the power of the Lord's Supper to communicate the meaning of the death of Jesus. I urged them to reenact the Lord's Supper more frequently because it was mandated by the Lord and because it takes us to the heart of God's story. One minister, moved by the emphasis I gave to the Lord's Supper, said this, "I really liked what you said about the Lord's Supper. We do it at our church once a year—on New Year's Eve. I don't think my people would be interested in doing it more often than that. Could you suggest a ritual that my people would embrace that would have the same effect?" Of course I was stunned, and I assured him that no ritual could replace the Lord's Supper.

A second example of reenactment found in biblical worship is the *Hebrew Passover and its fulfillment in the Christian Passover.* Most who read these words have probably been involved in a Christianized form of the Passover, but few Protestants (most readers of this text) are acquainted with the Great Paschal Vigil. The origins of the Vigil are found in 1 Corinthians 5:7–8: "For Christ, our Passover lamb, has been sacrificed. Therefore let us keep the Festival." Christians apparently marked the date of the death of Christ with a yearly festival from the very beginnings of the church.

A survey of the development of the Christian Passover is too complicated for the scope of this book. It was connected with the newly converted and the catechumenate process of incorporating them into the full life of the church. The culminating service, known as the Great Paschal Vigil, was an all-night service that began at dark on the eve of Easter and ended in the early morning of Easter Sunday. This service includes four parts woven together in a great reenactment of the events of the death and resurrection of Jesus and the believer's incorporation into his death and resurrection on our behalf and for the life of the world. The four parts of the Great Paschal Vigil are:

1. The Service of the Light
   The lighting of the fire is a vision of the resurrection.
2. The Service of Readings
   Readings of the story of God from creation, fall, God's involvement with Israel, and the incarnation of God in our history in Jesus Christ.
3. The Service of Baptism
   As the sun began to rise in the East, New Christians who had gone through the catechetical process of being discipled into Jesus were baptized into his death and resurrection.

53

4. The Easter Eucharist

>   Proclaiming Christ's resurrection from the dead, the church gathered to celebrate the Lord's Supper, the joyful Eucharist of his resurrection.

A third example of reenactment correspondence between Hebrew and early Christian worship is found in the *Hebrew and Christian way of marking time.* Time was understood in the Hebrew faith in daily, weekly, and yearly moments of divine significance and action. Jewish daily prayers are ordered around evening and morning. In the development of daily prayer in the Christian tradition, prayers are also ordered around evening and morning, which bracket the prayers that recall the enactment of the death and resurrection. The weekly worship of the Hebrew Sabbath was also taken up by the church. Saturday, of course, is the day of rest for the Hebrews. God has completed his work of creation in six days, and on the seventh, he rests. But Christian worship is on Sunday, the first day of the week, a working day in the Hebrew way of accounting time. Why do most Christians worship on Sunday and not Saturday? Two reasons: First, it is the day of the resurrection. Second, it is the day of re-creation. The resurrection signals a new beginning, a new creation, a new start. For this reason ancient Christians called Sunday the *eighth day*. It combines the first day of God's creation and the seventh day when he rested from his first creation. In the minds of early Christians the first day (creation typology) and the seventh day (Sabbath typology) were the eighth day, the day when God re-created, beginning his work of restoration and reclaiming the world.

The Hebrews also had a way of marking yearly time. These reenactments all celebrated God's presence in Israel's life and include such events as Rosh Hashanah (the first day of the year), Yom Kippur (the Day of Atonement), Hag Hassukkot (Feast of Booths), Pesach (Passover), and Hag Shauu'ot (Pentecost). Christians follow the Jewish principle of marking time through God's saving events. The Christian year, which developed in the first few centuries of the church, marked yearly time by Advent (waiting for the Messiah), Christmas (the Messiah has come), Epiphany (the Messiah is manifested to be for the whole world), Lent (preparing

54

for the death of Jesus), Holy Week (reenacting the final week and saving events), Easter (celebrating the resurrection), Ascension (Jesus ascends in glory to intercede for us at the right hand of the Father), and Pentecost (the coming of the Holy Spirit in a new way).

Not only have I demonstrated in a brief way that biblical worship *remembers* the story of God's saving deeds in history, but I have also shown that the two primary ways remembrance happens is through *historical recitation* and *dramatic reenactment*. However, these actions are not to be seen as mere incidences of information or dramatic skits. Rather they are powerful proclamations and enactments of life-giving engagements with the God who acts in history to save his creation and creatures.

Summary

In this chapter I have addressed the question: *How* does worship do God's story? I have answered that question by pointing to the biblical theme of *remembrance*. Worship remembers God's story through historical recitation and dramatic reenactment. We sing, preach, recite, and enact the story of God's great deeds of salvation. This theme is found repeatedly in Scripture from the very beginnings of worship in the time of Noah, in all of Israel's worship, in the church's worship, and in the eternal worship of the heavens.

Remembrance of God's saving deeds, however, does not exhaust biblical worship. There is another dimension of God's story that worship also does—*worship anticipates the future and the reign of Jesus over a re-created universe*. This is the subject of the next chapter.

3

Worship *Anticipates* the Future

God has a future for his world. Therefore, the whole story of God is not contained completely in past events. The Sunday school child knows this. God is working in past and present events to bring about this future. In theological language we call interest in the future *eschatology.* The Greek word *eschaton* means "future" and *ology* is "the study of." So *eschatology* is the study of future events.

I was in seminary during the middle of the twentieth century. At that time *eschatology* meant the charting out of the end-time events, the rapture, the second coming, the battle of Armageddon, and all the issues that cluster around what are called *the last days.* There certainly is a continued interest in these matters, as shown by the popularity of the *Left Behind* series and the current political issues centering around the Middle East. However, if asked, "What does eschatology have to do with worship?" most people would probably answer, "You preach about it in worship." And that, of course, is true. But only in part.

The eschatological nature of worship is more than preaching a sermon on future events. The content of eschatological worship has to do with God's rescue of the entire created order and the establishment of his rule over all heaven and earth. The eschato-logical nature of worship has to do with that *place* and *time* when God's rule is being done *on earth as it is in heaven*.

Worship remembers the past. Yes. But it always connects the past with the future. God acts in history in order to restore his kingdom. Worship makes this connection between past and present because worship celebrates God's saving deeds in the past that culminate in the future.[1]

To hope in the future is to explore God's purposes in history and *envision* a world at peace, the garden restored, and heaven and earth under the rule of God. We must go deep into the recollection of those saving events in order to see God's future vision. Then we must turn to God's vision for the world and ask, "How does worship birth within us a confidence and hope that the desert will be conquered and bloom once again?"

Certainly each of us can point to images that we have experienced in song, preaching, and communion that point to the hope that lies ahead. How many of us have heard stories of friends and relatives gathering around a deathbed to sing, "When the trumpet of the Lord shall sound and time shall be no more"? Who among us has not heard a local pastor at a funeral talk about life after death? And, of course, at the Lord's Supper we hear, "For whenever you eat this bread and drink this cup, *you proclaim the Lord's death until he comes*" (1 Cor. 11:26, emphasis added).

However, there is a depth to the biblical story that goes much deeper than an occasional or even a frequent reference to heaven and the believer's place in the eternal heavens. In this chapter I want to uncover how God reveals his vision for the world through our worship and see in these revelations the greater depth of God's vision. I can do no more than introduce the subject because an explanation of hope as an essential feature of the Triune story of God and of the worship of God is far beyond the scope of this writing.

How God's Vision for Creation Is Anticipated

The place to begin a study of God's vision for the world is in the Genesis account of creation. In the story of God's activity on each day of creation, we find a vision of how the world once was and what the world will once again become. Between the account of creation and re-creation lie the fall and, of course, God's work in Jesus Christ to rescue and restore the world, fulfilling God's original vision for creation and creatures.

The first and most obvious implication of the Genesis description of creation is that the universe is made by *divine* choice. *Who* makes the world is the primary issue. It is God who acts to make light, to separate the waters, to make dry ground appear, to cause the land to produce vegetation, to separate the day from the night, to make the fish of the sea and the birds of the air, to make the animals, to create man and woman, and finally to rest.

The emphasis on the *divine* as Creator is of utmost importance, not only during biblical times but also today. *False religions, then and now, separate the Creator from the Redeemer.* In this separation the Creator is made the source of evil in the world. This way of thinking separates the Redeemer from the Creator—the Redeemer is pitted against the Creator. In this dualistic scenario redemption is always a Gnostic form of salvation that releases one *out of this world*. In biblical faith, the Redeemer saves the creation. Creation is not intrinsically evil; it is God's beautiful handiwork spoiled by the effects of evil. God the Creator delivers his own creation from the ravages of sin and remakes it. Deliverance is *for the sake of the world*.

Much of today's spirituality is a *revival of the separation between the creator God and redeemer God*. In ancient Gnosticism as in New Age spirituality the spiritual life is always an escape, never a calling to live in this world in obedience to God's purposes for the world.

Unlike the Gnostics, the Christian faith does not separate the Creator and Redeemer into two Gods. There is only one God who both creates and redeems. The Apostles' Creed, whose origin lies in the battle of the early Christians with the Gnostics, rejects Gnostic dualism and affirms the unity of Creator and Redeemer in its first twelve words, "I believe in God the Father Almighty, *maker* of heaven and earth." To affirm that the creation is made by the *divine* is profound because it confesses the divine beginnings of the world and affirms that God's vision for the world is first set forth in the liturgy of creation (Genesis 1–3). Creation itself reveals a divine origin and purpose for the material order of things that God himself has made.

The *divine* beginnings of creation cannot be fully appreciated until they are connected with a second word of creation, design. The world in which we live, made by God, is not a world of chaos and meaninglessness; it is a world of order. Creation therefore reveals design. The creation stories describe the purposes and intention of *divine design.* God, who creates a world to work in harmony, called into existence a humanity shaped by his design and a created order according to his design. Everything in creation has a place, a function, and a meaning. The inhabitants of the world are to work according to a design mandated by God. Human beings are called to live in continuity with God's purposes. Those who turn their back on God and live according to their own whims and fancies disrupt God's intentions and pervert God's purposes for his creation.

If the creation liturgy expresses a *divine design* to the whole created order, what does that say about worship? It says that worship is not thrown together, but that it too, like the rest of creation, is ordered and reflects the divine design. For us, it means that worship should do God's narrative and point to the future when creation, delivered from sin, will be restored to God's original design. In this world there is always a witness to the restoration of the world, and you should be able to find it in the worship of the church.

Just to know *worship should envision God's future for history and for the world* opens windows to view what we do in worship in a new way. Worship is world-building, for it displays the work of re-creation, which God accomplishes with his own two hands—the incarnate Word and the Holy Spirit.

How God's Vision for the World Is Continually Anticipated in Worship

The purpose of the Genesis account of creation is *doxology* (right praise); it calls us to a posture of praise. Doxology is our response to God's story. It receives God's story as God's way of disclosing his intention for creation. So Christian creation doxology is a way of knowing and affirming God's way in the world. Doxology is the way to momentarily experience the eternal kingdom of God's perfection over all creation.

This vision of the world, first revealed to us in the Genesis liturgy, now becomes continually recast in worship. When worship remembers the past, it praises God for God's work in history whereby he has already begun the restoration of the world. When worship anticipates the future, it looks for the culmination of all God's works in the complete transformation of the world, the consummation of God's work in Jesus Christ by the power of the Spirit, whereby worship witnesses to the victory of Christ over all the powers and principalities and proclaims he now rules over all creation as the Lord of the universe.

Consider this: The vision of God opens with the liturgy of creation in which God sets forth his purposes for the world. The world is to be his theater of glory. God inhabits the world. God has intimate fellowship with his creatures; he calls them to care for the earth, to open the treasures of creation, and to cooperate with him in culture-making, in establishing civilization, in populating the world, and in making the world a habitation of God's splendor and glory.

On the other hand, the vision of God culminates in a glorious picture of the garden restored. All creation is at rest. The harmony and design of God's initial creative purposes are now vividly displayed everywhere. The book of Revelation, like the Genesis liturgy, is a liturgy to the future of God's world. It is not a book whose primary purpose is to deliver historical or scientific information; it is a book of doxological praise. It is a worship book!

For example, every covenant made with Israel is a worship event. Read the creation account as a liturgical event in which God covenants with the earth and with his creatures to establish the earth and human community under the divine design.

Since the fall, all Israel's covenants and all the worship that proceeds from these covenants call attention to God's intent for the world. Worship continually holds up God's vision of a new heaven and earth and an eternal community of God's people living in fellowship with God, doing God's will on earth, walking in God's ways, and fulfilling the vision of creation.

61

In the vision of the world in all of Israel's worship we see the world to come. The tabernacle and temple rites reveal the sacrificial way that God opens the window of heaven. Passover reveals his redemption, the Day of Atonement his forgiveness. The Torah reveals how one is to live righteously and with justice now in this world in anticipation of the world to come.

In the new covenant in Jesus Christ, one sees how God is going to bring his vision for the world to fruition. Jesus Christ by his sacrifice over sin has won a great victory over the powers of evil. Worship sings, the Scriptures proclaim, the Eucharist enacts, and the Christian year tells forth the vision of God for this world. It tells how he has conquered all the forces of evil—those principalities and powers that continually seek to bring ruin against his divine design. It tells how Christ has overcome these powers by his cross and resurrection. It tells how he has established a new beginning for history and for his world. It celebrates the victory of Christ over sin and death and extols Jesus Christ for reestablishing the vision first put forth in the liturgy of creation. In this way, in both the worship of Israel and in the worship of the church, the vision of God for the world is to be made known. We turn now to a few specific examples.

The Sabbath Anticipates God's Vision for the World

The creation liturgy presents an orderly world, a ritual world, and a relational world. The place where these themes of God's design come together is in the Sabbath.

For example, I have had the good fortune to have a friendship with an Orthodox Jew. He is on the liberal side of the orthodox way of life by dress and behavior; nevertheless, he stands in the historic spiritual traditions of the Jewish community—keeping a Kosher house, he observes all the feasts and festivals and weekly attendance to Jewish rituals including the Sabbath.

On one occasion when I was at his home, he put his arm on my shoulder, looked me in the eye, and said, "Bob, do you know why the Jews love the Sabbath so much?"

"Well," I said, "I am not sure what to say."

"The Sabbath," he said, "is all about relationship. Relationship with God, with our community of faith, with our families—spouses, children, grandchildren—relationship with nature and the beauty of God. We do no work of any kind for a full day. We spend our time eating (food prepared the day before), listening to good music, and going to the synagogue."

What he was saying to me is, "The Sabbath anticipates our eternal rest."

Temple Space Anticipates God's Vision for the World

A little-known point about Old Testament worship is that the future is visualized in the architecture of the space. One can walk into the worship space and be filled with awe at the sight of God's future world where his glory fills heaven and earth.

For example, I received the following email from one of my Northern Seminary students, Barb Stellwagen. In these few words she captures how God's majesty and glory can be experienced in the space where we worship:

> Jim and I just returned from Austria where we saw lots of incredibly beautiful and ornate cathedrals. There had been a time when I would've looked at them and thought it all a waste . . . beautiful . . . but I would've thought that it was all empty religion. Since taking your class, I look at it differently. When I went in the cathedrals, it really gave me the sense of preparing for worship. It reminded me that I was entering the presence of the King of Kings. It created awe in my spirit for the One who alone is worthy to receive all of this honor. In Austria, having seen the palaces of kings and emperors and all the grandeur they claim for themselves, it seemed fitting that the "dwelling" of the King of Kings ought to be grand and beautiful. The huge portraits that depicted the biblical stories brought it all to life, and I found myself drawn into worship without even being able to understand the German words at all.
>
> One day in Innsbruck, Austria, we were at a cathedral just before the Mass was to begin and the little choir, accompanied by guitar, was leading worship. The tour director had the nerve to lead our group right up to the front of the cathedral, as the congregants were preparing for worship in the pews. She stood there explaining the details of the sanctuary, seemingly oblivious to the worship that

was beginning all around her. I stood to the side, embarrassed, as our group took pictures and talked to one another in the front of the cathedral. I felt like we were violating the worship. As I leaned against one of the massive pillars, I tried to ignore our group and focus on the singers. As I listened to the music echo through the incredible space, I was overcome by the beauty and the majesty of God himself, and I wept. I didn't want to leave that place. As we went outside, the bells in the tower began to ring out the call to gather the faithful (it was incredibly loud and joyful), and later I learned that it was a special service to pray that young people would join the church.

Anyway, all that to say thank you for opening my eyes to the beauty of icons and liturgical worship and the importance of creating a sense of awe in our worship space.[2]

There is no missing the point!

Greg Beale, professor of New Testament studies at Wheaton College, writes about how the tabernacle and temple of the Jewish tradition are designed to symbolically point to the presence of God in all creation. He also points out that chapter 12 of John's Revelation pictures the new heavens and new earth as the eschatological temple. The temple, the space of Old Testament worship, is a continual reminder of God's goal for the creation—a renewed and restored creation that fulfills in every way the cosmic goal of history worked out by God together with his Son and Spirit. The temple stands within Israel as a provocative testimony to what God is doing in time and space to bring about his purposes on earth. Greg Beale writes that the temple is a "microcosm of the entire heaven and earth."[3]

> Our thesis is that Israel's temple was composed of three main parts, each of which symbolized a major part of the cosmos: 1) The outer court represented the habitable world where humanity dwelt; 2) the holy place was emblematic of the visible heavens and its light source; 3) the holy of holies symbolized the invisible direction of the cosmos where God and his heavenly hosts dwelt.[4]

These three fundamental divisions—the outer court, the inner court, and the Holy of Holies represent the whole of God's cosmos:

the outer represents the natural earth; the inner court is the symbol of the visible eye; the Holy of Holies represents the invisible parts of the cosmos. "Israel's temple was a small model of the heaven and earth, which points to the end-time goal of God's presence dwelling throughout the creation and no longer only in the back room of the temple."[5] Consequently, "the understanding of the temple as a small model of the entire cosmos is part of a larger perspective in which the temple pointed forward to a huge world-wide sanctuary in which God's presence would dwell in every part of the cosmos. . . . John later pictures the entire new heavens and new earth to be one mammoth temple in which God dwells as God formerly dwelt in the holy of holies."[6]

In the beauty of the temple God keeps before his people the vision of the new heavens and new earth. Historic Christian churches have also kept God's vision alive in their worship space. Unfortunately the modern and contemporary church has, for the most part, disregarded God's cosmic vision and has reduced space to a utilitarian usage. Now that we live in a more visual period of history, younger leaders in particular are rediscovering how space speaks and are looking once again to the rediscovery of biblical and historical worship.

Holy Living Anticipates God's Vision for the World

Worship and holy living are always brought together in God's covenant, old and new. For example, one of my favorite Scripture passages on worship is 1 Peter 2:9–10: "But you are a chosen people, a royal priesthood, a holy nation, a people belonging to God, that you may declare the praises of him who called you out of darkness into his wonderful light." This passage has eschatological overtones— and when it is read together with other worship passages, it speaks of the ultimate deliverance of all God's people from the power of sin and death.

But this clear passage on worship not only points to the future reign of God over all things but also leads the worshiper directly into holy living, which is to be a direct outcome of worship and an anticipation of life in God's eschatological domain. "Dear friends," Paul writes as an immediate follow-up to his instruction on worship,

"I urge you as aliens and strangers in the world, to abstain from sinful desires, which war against your soul. Live such good lives among the pagans that, though they accuse you of doing wrong, they may see your good deeds and glorify God on the day he visits us" (1 Peter 2:11–12). Not only does worship point to the culmination of all history in the new heavens and new earth, but it also shapes the ethical behavior of God's people to reflect kingdom ethics here on earth. Consequently, the ethical life of the church is an eschatological witness to the world of how people should be living and how the world will be under the reign of God.

Conclusion

In both chapters 2 and 3 I have introduced how God's vision for the world is remembered and anticipated in worship. Worship is all about how God, with his own two hands—the incarnate Word and the Holy Spirit—has rescued the world. The biblical God is an active God—he creates, becomes active in the world to rescue his creation from sin and death, and restores the world to paradise and beyond in the new heavens and new earth. The centerpiece of his saving action is the incarnation, death, and resurrection, where sin and death have been defeated and where the deliverance of creatures and creation, which will be consummated at the end of history, will begin.

In the meantime, worship is the witness to this vision. In worship we *remember* God's redemptive work in history. We especially remember the story of Israel and how it is a type of the Christ event, pointing to the saving events surrounding the life, ministry, death, and resurrection of Jesus Christ. We also *anticipate* the future. Worship connects the past with the future, for it is here in worship where God recasts his original vision. However, a worship that casts God's vision for his world appears to have become lost in many of our churches.

How the *Fullness* of God's Story Became Lost

When I talk to my classes or to small groups, the biblical information on worship simply doesn't seem to be grasped quickly. I had one excellent student who, after three semesters of worship studies, came to me and said, "It took me three semesters to understand what you are talking about, and it has revolutionized my ministry."

Why do people have such trouble grasping the theology of ancient worship? I think one reason is because we tend to be New Testament Christians rather than Bible Christians. We disregard Old Testament worship instructions because we regard the Old Testament to be fulfilled in Jesus. Therefore, we don't read the Bible as God's whole story. We don't connect the creation liturgy with God's purposes for the world, so we don't pay attention to how God is working in history to redeem and rescue the whole world and fulfill his creation vision. This was the problem with the Gnostic heresy in the ancient church—they rejected the entire Old Testament. We have not rejected the Old Testament, but we have, at the very least, ignored the creation story of God's vision and overlooked how God's purposes were being worked out in Israel.

In order to more fully grasp how God's vision was lost in worship, I will concentrate in this chapter on a very brief survey of worship in the five Western paradigms of history—the ancient, medieval, Reformation, modern, and contemporary. In each of these paradigms, we will search for evidence of a worship that *remembers* God's saving action in the past and *anticipates* the completion of God's final victory over sin and death in his coming again to establish his rule over all the heavens and the earth.

Worship and God's Vision in the Ancient Church

The ancient church is generally dated to AD 600, the year that many hold to be the definitive end of the Roman Empire. Many Protestant Christians tend to dismiss the ancient fathers and their insights, saying they were fallible human beings so we don't need to pay any attention to them. They were, of course, subject to cultural influence, even as we are. However, their contributions were vast and fundamental. They brought us the Apostles' Creed, the Nicene Creed (AD 325), and the Chalcedon Creed (AD 451), which affirm God's story of creation, incarnation, and re-creation. These creeds affirm the biblical teaching that Jesus is the God-man. They affirm the ancient axiom that it is "only God who saves" (thus Jesus is God) and "only that which God became is healed" (that Jesus is man). Not only do they clarify the issues pertaining to Christ's deity and to salvation through God who became man, but they also established the canon of Scripture and rules for biblical interpretation. In addition, they determined the shape of the liturgy and handed down ethical teaching consistent with biblical thought.

The liberal theologians of the last century argued that ancient Christianity was formed by an adaptation of Hellenistic ideas. They dismissed the creeds and stripped Jesus of his supernatural character. Actually they removed the supernatural entirely and viewed Jesus as an unusual person—perhaps a prophet—but no more. Consequently, liberals rejected the vision of God that is clearly the fundamental content of ancient Christian worship.

68

However, recent scholars recognize that the major influence on the ancient fathers is not Hellenistic ideas, but the Old Testament itself.

I will illustrate the sensitivity to *whole-Bible worship* with a couple examples from the *Apostolic Constitutions*. The *Constitutions* make up the largest body of liturgical material from the ancient church. It claims to have originated from the second century, but in fact it reflects a number of liturgical documents from the *Apostolic Tradition of Hippolytus* to the *Didascalia of the Apostles* to the so-called Clementine Liturgy. The *Apostolic Constitutions* first appeared about AD 380 in Syria or Constantinople. This is about the same time that Augustine began his ministry.

The work is far too long to present here. I will therefore concentrate on the two aspects of biblical worship presented previously—remembrance and anticipation.

Remembrance in Ancient Christian Worship

I have already commented on the battle the ancient church fathers had with the Gnostics over the Old Testament. For the Gnostics, the Old Testament God, Yahweh, was an altogether different God from the God of the New Testament. The God of the Old Testament was not only inferior, he was also evil and the source of evil in the world. Yahweh was the creator of the material world, and therefore all things material were evil, including the human body. Only that which was invisible and of the spirit was good. Therefore, you will never find mention of God working in the history of Israel in any of the Gnostic liturgies.

Contrary to the Gnostic outright rejection of the Old Testament, the ancient fathers thoroughly affirm Yahweh as the same God as the Father of our Lord Jesus Christ. All ancient theology and liturgies reflect this conviction and therefore always emphasize the working of God in history among the patriarchs and in Israel. For this reason the liturgies of those faithful to the tradition of the apostles will be filled with references to God's work in Old Testament times. In this prayer from Anthony the Patriarch, contained in the worship resources from the *Apostolic Constitutions*, note the emphasis on remembering God's saving deeds in the past:

69

For, from the beginning, when our father Abraham
undertook to walk in the way of truth,
thou didst reveal thyself to him and guide him,
thou didst teach him the true nature of the present age.
His faith preceded his knowledge,
and the Covenant accompanied his faith.
For thou didst tell him:
"I will multiply thy descendants
like the stars in heaven,
like the sand on the sea-shore."

So too, in giving him Isaac
whose life, according to thy designs,
was to be like to his own,
thou didst proclaim thyself his God, saying:
"I will be thy God
and the God of thy descendants after thee."

So too again, when our father Jacob
set out for Mesopotamia,
thou didst tell him, showing him the Messiah:
"Behold, I am with thee.
I will increase and multiply thy posterity."

To Moses also, thy faithful servant,
thou didst say, in the vision of the bush:
"I am who I am.
Such is my name which is to be remembered."

Defender of the descendants of Abraham,
blessed be thou through the ages.[1]

In many of our churches today there is a neglect of remembrance in worship. It arises from the loss of attention to the whole Bible. A shift has taken place toward a focus on therapeutic or inspirational preaching and to the rise of entertainment or presentational worship. Pastors and church leaders would do well to return to the Scriptures and be more faithful to the biblical emphasis on remembrance that is found in the ancient liturgies of the church. One does not need to become liturgical to become more biblical in worship. Remembrance of God's actions in history to save the world can be effectively done in a spontaneous way as well. When planning worship ask, "Does the service connect creation with God's involvement in the history of Israel, with his incarnation, death, resurrection, ascension, eternal intercession, and coming again to establish his rule over all creation?" If you can answer "Yes" to that question, you are well on your way into worship that has the biblical content of remembrance and anticipation.

Anticipation in Ancient Christian Worship

I will turn again to the *Apostolic Constitutions* for an example of worship that anticipates the consummation of history under the reign of Jesus Christ. This time we will look at a portion of the liturgy that is done by the catechumens who have recently been baptized. This confessional prayer reflects the training these catechumenates have received over the previous three years. It sweeps from creation to incarnation and into the kingdom that is to come. It also reflects the convictions of the Nicene Creed, which was written in AD 325 but not completely confirmed by the church until the Council of Constantinople in AD 380.

> I believe and I have been baptised,
> In the one, the uncreated, the only true God almighty, Father of Christ, who created and made all things and "from whom all things come,"
> And in Jesus Christ the Lord, his only-begotten Son, "First born of every creature,"
> who was begotten, not created, before the ages, according to the Father's good pleasure,
> "through whom all things were made," those in heaven and those on earth, the visible and the invisible,
> who, in the last times, came down from heaven, was incarnate and was born of Mary, the holy virgin,
> who lived a holy life according to the law of his God and Father,
> who suffered under Pontius Pilate and died for us,
> who, after his passion, was raised from the dead on the third day,

who ascended into heaven and sits at the right hand of the
Father,
who will come again with glory at the consummation of the age,
to judge the living and the dead, whose kingdom has no end.
I have been baptised also in the Holy Spirit, the Paraclete, who
assists all the saints from the beginning of the world,
whom the Father sent to the Apostles, according to the promise
of our Saviour and Lord Jesus Christ,
whom he has sent since then to all those who believe in the holy
catholic and apostolic Church,
and in the resurrection of the flesh,
in the forgiveness of sins,
in the Kingdom of heaven and in the life of the age to come.[2]

A brief review of this confession doxology demonstrates that the
full story of God is there in outline form. The confession is marked by
the Triune structure of God's story. The Trinity is not mentioned as a
mere isolated fact but is set forth with its dynamic activity and inter-
relationship. The Father creates; the Son becomes involved in creation
through incarnation, death, resurrection, ascension, intercession, and
coming again in glory to set up his kingdom forever. The Holy Spirit
is involved in the whole rescue mission of God, assisting the saints,
empowering the apostles and the church, and witnessing to the resurrection of the flesh, the forgiveness of sin, and the kingdom to come. It
doesn't get any clearer than that. And this is only a *summary* of what
these new Christians have prayerfully studied for three years.

The Vision of God in Eastern and Western Medieval Liturgies

Eastern and Western liturgies each developed their own form
of worship, although both remained faithful to their basic roots in
ancient worship, especially in their continuance of Word and Eucharist as the basic structure of worship. Although there are many
instances of mutual influence between the traditions, it can be said
that Carthage and Rome are the mother churches of the West and
Jerusalem, Antioch, and Alexandria are the root churches for the
Eastern tradition.

Eastern Churches

Eventually the Eastern liturgies were shaped by worship in Constantinople, especially the liturgies of St. Basil and St. John Chrysostom. These liturgies were highly complex by comparison to the liturgies of the second and third centuries. A chief emphasis of the Eastern liturgies has always been mystery. The Eastern Church dwells on the mystery of the paradoxes in God's story. God is at once invisible, incomprehensible, and infinite, yet in the incarnation, God is visible and knowable. Eastern liturgies are also very colorful with vestments, genuflections, frequent use of the sign of the cross, flowery language, and numerous repetitions. Eastern liturgies follow the emphasis of ancient liturgies in their focus on Christ as the victor over sin and death and on the resurrection with the promise that all things will be made new.

One striking feature of the Eastern liturgy is its emphasis on anticipation. Again and again the liturgy invites the worshipers to enter into the heavenlies to join in the worship of the heavenly throng. There are many examples of the heavenly worship from which to choose. Below is the Anaphora from the St. Basil Liturgy. A careful reading will demonstrate the story of God and the vision of eternal worship in the re-created world.

> (*in a low voice*) O truly existing One, Master, Lord, God, almighty and adorable Father, how right it is, and befitting the majesty of Your holiness, to praise You, to sing to You, to bless You, to worship You, and to glorify You. You alone are truly God, and we offer You this spiritual worship with a humble spirit and a contrite heart. You have given us the knowledge of Your truth. Who is worthy to speak of Your mighty deeds, or make all Your praises heard? O Master of all things, Lord of heaven and earth, and of all creation, both visible and invisible, You are seated upon the throne of glory and behold the depths. You are without beginning, invisible, incomprehensible, indescribable, changeless. O Father of our Lord Jesus Christ, the great God and Savior, our Hope, Who is the image of Your goodness, the seal equal to its model, Who shows You in Himself: the Father, Living Word, true God before all ages, Wisdom, Life, Sanctification, Power, true Light: Through You the Holy Spirit was manifested, the Spirit of truth, the gift of adoption, the pledge of our future inheritance, the first-fruits of eternal good things, the

life-giving Power, the fountain of holiness; through Whom every rational and spiritual creature is made capable to worship You and give You eternal glorification, for all things are Your servants. You are praised by the angels, the archangels, the thrones, the dominions, the principalities, the authorities, the powers, and the many-eyed cherubim. The seraphim are around You, each having six wings: with two they veil their face, with two their feet, and with two they fly, continually crying out to one another with mouths that do not grow tired, in praises which are never silent,

(*aloud*) singing, proclaiming, shouting the hymn of victory:

Holy! Holy! Holy! Lord of Hosts! Heaven and earth are filled with Your glory. Hosanna in the highest! Blessed is He Who comes in the Name of the Lord! Hosanna in the highest![3]

Western Churches

The Western liturgies are very heavily influenced by Roman worship, which shares the underlying structure of Word and Eucharist but has a style that is quite different from that of the Eastern Church. The style of Roman worship is much more legalistic and rigid. Until recently (Vatican II, 1963) Roman worship was always done in Latin, even though Latin was not the language of the celebrating church. For most Protestants, the Roman liturgy is too liturgical and rote; by comparison to the Eastern liturgies, the Roman liturgy is quite dull.

While the Eastern emphasizes the mysteries of God in the heavens made visible on earth through the Word, signs, and sounds of worship, the emphasis of the Roman Mass focused on the eucharistic sacrifice. By the late medieval period the service of the Word with preaching was infrequent. The Mass was generally reduced to the eucharistic prayers. Because the Word was dropped and the focus on the Mass centered on the death of Christ, the whole story of God was not proclaimed in worship. The story was reduced to the death of Christ, his suffering, and the salvation that was brought through the sacraments.

The portion of the Roman Mass below is the offertory, the prayer at the beginning of the Eucharist. Note in particular the frequent references to the sacrifice of Christ, the focal point of the Mass.

Unfortunately *God's full vision for the re-creation of the world is at best muted and at worst ignored.*

> *Celebrant:* The Lord be with you.
> *Server:* And with you.
> *Celebrant:* Let us pray.
> *He now takes the paten with the host, which he offers up, saying:*
> Holy Father, almighty, everlasting God, accept this unblemished sacrificial offering, which I, thy unworthy servant, make to thee, my living and true God, for my countless sins, offences, and neglects, and on behalf of all who are present here; likewise for all believing Christians, living and dead. Accept it for their good and mine, so that it may save us and bring us to everlasting life. Amen.
> *Moving to the Epistle side, the priest now pours wine and water into the chalice. He blesses the water, saying:*
> O God, by whom the dignity of human nature was wondrously established and yet more wondrously restored, grant that through the sacramental use of this water and wine we may have fellowship in the Godhead of him who deigned to share our manhood, Jesus Christ, thy Son, our Lord, who is God, living and reigning with thee in the unity of the Holy Spirit, for ever and ever. Amen.
> *He returns to the middle of the altar and offers up the chalice, saying:*
> We offer thee, Lord, the chalice of salvation, entreating thy mercy that our offering may ascend with a sweet fragrance in the presence of thy divine majesty for our salvation and for that of all the world. Amen.
> *Bowing slightly, he continues:*
> Humbled in spirit and contrite of heart, may we find favour with thee, Lord, and may our sacrifice be so offered in thy sight this day that it may please thee, Lord our God.
> *He then stands erect and invokes the Holy Spirit, making the sign of the cross over the bread and wine:*
> Come, thou sanctifier, almighty, everlasting God, and bless these sacrificial gifts, prepared for the glory of thy holy name.
> *The priest now goes to the Epistle side, where he washes his hands, reciting Psalm 25:6–12:*
> With the pure in heart, I will wash my hands clean and take my place among them at thy altar, Lord, listening there to the sound of thy praises, telling the story of all thy wonderful deeds. How well, Lord, I love thy house in its beauty, the place where thy own glory

dwells! Lord, never count this soul for lost with the wicked, this life among the bloodthirsty: hands ever stained with guilt, palms ever itching for a bribe! Be it mine to guide my steps clear of wrong: deliver me in thy mercy. My feet are set on firm ground; where thy people gather, Lord, I will join in blessing thy name.

The Gloria Patri *is omitted in the Masses of Passiontide and of the Dead.*

Glory be to the Father, and to the Son, and to the Holy Ghost. As it was in the beginning, is now, and ever shall be, world without end. Amen.

Then, returning to the middle of the altar, the priest says:

Holy Trinity, accept the offering we here make to thee in memory of the passion, resurrection, and ascension of our Lord Jesus Christ; in honour, too, of blessed Mary, ever-virgin, of blessed John the Baptist, of the holy apostles Peter and Paul, of the Martyrs whose relics are here, and of all the saints. To them let it bring honour, to us salvation; and may they whom we are commemorating on earth graciously plead for us in heaven: through the same Christ our Lord. Amen.

He now says one or more Secret prayers. Their number and order are those of the Collects. At the end of the last he says aloud:

Celebrant: For ever and ever.

Server: Amen.[4]

In brief, Eastern and Western worship differed in content, structure, and style. The content of Eastern worship maintained a strong resemblance to the narrative of ancient worship, emphasizing creation, incarnation, and re-creation in the pattern of Word and sacrament. Western worship, on the other hand, reduced the full content of God's story to a focus on the sacrifice of Christ for sin. They dropped the preached Word, the verbal proclamation of God's story! The style (music and the arts) reflected the Roman influence in the West and the Byzantine culture in the East.

The Vision of God in the Reformation Liturgies

The Reformation and its changes in worship always need to be understood in the context of its sharp theological and liturgical critique of Western Roman Catholic worship. The Reformation was primarily a recovery of the authority of Scripture along with a rejection of the Roman tradition, the institutional church, the canons and creeds of later medievalism, and Roman focus on the Mass as a sacrifice of Christ.

In worship, three positions were espoused. The Lutheran and Anglican Churches retained much of the Catholic Mass, whereas the Anabaptists threw out the Mass in favor of the meal of fellowship. The Reformed churches took a middle road, simplifying the liturgical elements and structure of the Mass. The distinct contribution to worship by all three branches of the Reformation is that they restored Scripture reading and preaching to the rightful place it had in the ancient church.

There is one noted shift in Reformation worship from the ancient liturgies of the church: *worship now places greater attention on the individual's condition before God.* The vision of God to reclaim the whole world and redeem all flesh and matter through the victory of Christ over sin and death scarcely appears (although it is found in the Lutheran liturgies). The Reformed liturgies continue to emphasize the sacrifice of Christ, not as a re-sacrifice as in the Roman liturgy, but Christ as a substitute for my sin. The work of Christ for the whole world is now beginning to be reduced to the sacrifice of Christ for the individual. The following quote comes from the preface to communion in Calvin's Strassburg Liturgy (1545). It was read to the people every time they gathered to receive the Lord's Supper.

> We have heard, my brethren, how our Lord observed His Supper with His disciples, from which we learn that strangers and those who do not belong to the company of His faithful people must not be admitted. Therefore, following that precept in the name and by the authority of our Lord Jesus Christ, I excommunicate all idolaters, blasphemers, and despisers of God, all heretics and those who create private sects in order to break the unity of the Church, all perjurers, all who rebel against father or mother or superior, all who promote sedition or mutiny; brutal and disorderly persons, adulterers, lewd and lustful men, thieves, ravishers, greedy and graspy people, drunkards, gluttons, and all those who lead a scandalous and dissolute life. I warn them to abstain from this Holy Table, lest they defile

and contaminate the holy food which our Lord Jesus Christ gives to none except they that belong to His household of faith.

Moreover, in accordance with the exhortation of St. Paul, let every man examine and prove his own conscience to see whether he truly repents of his faults and grieves over his sins, desiring to live henceforth a holy life according to God. Above all, let him see whether he has his trust in the mercy of God and seeks his salvation wholly in Jesus Christ and, renouncing all hatred and rancor, has high resolve and courage to live in peace and brotherly love with his neighbors.

If we have this witness in our hearts before God, never doubt that he claims us as His children, and that the Lord Jesus addresses His Word to us, to invite us to His Table and to give us this holy Sacrament which He imparted to His disciples.[5]

One can see the distinct shift taking place in this prayer as the focus is on the worthiness (or lack thereof) of an individual to receive communion. The prayer and types of prayer like it are called "fencing-in" prayers. They are admonitions to exclude nonbelievers and backslidden believers from coming to the Table. Prior to the Reformation all who had been baptized were admitted to the Table. From here on into the twentieth century the emphasis is "come to the Table if you have had a conversion experience and you are living the transformed life." At the same time, baptism has become increasingly unimportant in many churches of the "fall tradition."

The Vision of God in the Worship of the Modern World

The Reformation set into motion a wave of new church movements, one right after the other. Each movement had its own leader who stamped the new movement with a particular theology and its own convictions about worship. The one common emphasis among all these movements was the elevation of Scripture and preaching. It was also common for these groups to neglect the Lord's Supper, celebrating it infrequently in reaction to the Roman Catholic's nearly exclusive emphasis on worship as the eucharistic sacrifice.

From the seventeenth century through the nineteenth century there are two general movements of worship worth noting. They are worship as education and worship as experience. Neither of these approaches to worship proclaimed and enacted the *full* story of God's vision.

Worship as Education *(Seventeenth Century)*

The modern world (1750–1950) is a period of history vastly different from the ancient, the medieval, or the Reformation eras. It was a time of great change in knowledge and in the way of obtaining knowledge. Named the Enlightenment, this era produced the cosmological revolution, introduced reason and science as the method of discovering truth, and rejected the Christian conviction of truth known by revelation.

Protestant orthodoxy, which was strongly influenced by rationalism, emerged in the seventeenth century to defend revelation and teach God's truth from Scripture. Clergy were well versed in Greek and Hebrew, in biblical and systematic theology, and in the art of using logic to make a case for the Christian faith. The centerpiece of worship was the sermon, and the emphasis of the sermon was on knowing God's Word and defending its truth. Unfortunately, the zeal that fueled Reformation worship and preaching was gradually replaced by long, tedious, argumentative sermons. Protestant orthodoxy was replaced by a "dead orthodoxy," and the churches became empty.

There are a number of different seventeenth-century models of worship such as the Presbyterian, Congregational, and Baptist. The most influential form of worship was the Presbyterian model:

Order for the Service of the Word
Call to Worship
Prayer of Approach
Psalm Reading
Old Testament Chapter
New Testament Chapter
Psalm (sung)
Prayer before Sermon
Sermon

General Prayer
Lord's Prayer
Psalm (sung)

Order of the Lord's Supper (*four times a year*)
Exhortation
Warning
Invitation to the Table
Words of Institution
Prayer, Thanksgiving or Blessing of Bread and Wine
Fraction and Delivery
Exhortation
Solemn Thanksgiving
Collection for the Poor[6]

The Westminster Directory, a Presbyterian directory on worship, was published in 1643 and prescribed the order of worship above. It is difficult to determine its substance by looking at an outline. However, a study of the texts demonstrates that seventeenth-century worship does not emphasize remembrance and anticipation as in the narrative worship of the early church. Its emphasis is more on education. Preaching followed the *Lectio Continua* model, which presented series of sermons on various books of Scripture. Certainly in preaching, in reading the Psalms, in reading texts from both the Old and New Testaments, as well as the various exhortations, remembrance of God's work in the past and God's reign over creation in the future was mentioned. But the narrative nature of worship that ties together creation, incarnation, and re-creation was not obvious.

Baptists looked to the Bible for their worship and developed a variety of approaches to worship style. By the eighteenth century the Baptist style of worship converged into the following common pattern (1695):

Service of the Word
Psalm
Prayer

Scripture
Sermon(s)
Prayer

Lord's Supper (*once a month*)
Homily and Exhortation
Blessing the Bread
Words of Institution
Receiving the Bread
Blessing the Wine
Words of Institution
Receiving the Wine
Psalm (hymn)
Benediction[7]

The early Baptists, like the Presbyterians, were very much oriented toward growth in knowledge. Most people today think of Baptist worship as experiential, evangelistic, and spontaneous as opposed to orderly and intellectual, but the original Baptists of the seventeenth century were significantly more Reformed. Today there are many Baptists in England who reflect seventeenth-century style and content, and though little known, there is a group in America known as the Reformed Baptists. Most Baptists today follow a more spontaneous and experiential approach to worship, influenced by the later revivalistic movement.

In summary, if there is a failing in seventeenth-century worship, it is that, like the Enlightenment, the worship tended to emphasize facts without adequate interpretation. It pressed the arguments for the validity of the facts without adequately interpreting the story and vision of God working in creation to win back his world and reign over the entire creation as Lord.

Worship as Experience *(Eighteenth and Nineteenth Centuries)*

The entire landscape of worship was about to change as the church entered the eighteenth century. The Industrial Revolution resulted in a huge migration of workers to the city. Cities were crowded, and conditions were wretched with inadequate housing, poor sanitation, inadequate supplies of food and water, rampant poverty, crime, people living on the street, and disease and death at an all-time high.

In this situation the churches were ill equipped to address the needs of the people. They had been preoccupied with defending the faith, building arguments against the unbeliever, and pressing issues of truthfulness, which meant very little to the common person stuck in wretched living conditions with no apparent way out.

The romantic movement began to breed a class of people who rejected the validity of reason and emphasized the power of personal experience as validating truth. This emphasis, like the focus on reason that spawned educational worship, now resulted in experiential worship. This shift found expression in the great evangelical awakenings in the last half of the eighteenth century.

John Wesley (1703–1791) is the best-known figure of the evangelical awakening. However Wesley, himself an Anglican, remained faithful to the worship of the Anglican church all of his life. He reinvigorated the ancient liturgy, placing a strong emphasis on personal faith experienced in liturgy of Word and sacrament. He emphasized frequent communion, conversion, preaching, and enthusiastic hymn singing. (He wrote numerous hymns, including sixty-six eucharistic hymns, many of which are still sung today.) Wesley is the founder of the Methodist movement, which is known for its enthusiasm. Anglican worship is not an enthusiastic worship; it is done as prayer. Wesley, however, introduced enthusiastic preaching and singing, which Methodism took over as its distinguishing mark. There has always been a liturgical Methodism that reflects John Wesley's love of the Anglican liturgy, but for the most part, Methodism gravitated toward the more loose style of worship known as *revival worship.*

Revival worship drew from the field revivals of the Methodist frontier movement in America. Revivalism swept westward in the late eighteenth century. A revivalist would appear in a town—possibly a town without a church—set up a tent or some other kind of nonpermanent space, and hold a revival meeting. For the most part the revival meeting consisted of these parts:

Singing to warm the heart and soften the soul.

Preaching to proclaim the Good News of salvation in Christ.

Invitation to receive Jesus as the personal Lord and Savior of your life.

After the evangelist left town to preach somewhere else, the converted remained to begin their own church. The only model these new Christians had was the threefold model taught by the evangelist. Therefore they built churches and communities of faith based on the threefold model. This model was quite popular until the middle of the twentieth century, and it is still practiced today, especially in Southern fundamentalist churches.

The emphasis of these services is not on the God who creates and becomes involved with his creation in incarnation, death, and resurrection to re-create creatures and creation. Rather, the emphasis is on part of God's story and vision, because there is a strong piety expressed in preaching and hymns that focus on the death of Christ as the source of becoming a new creature and sustaining a personal relationship with the Lord. Important as that is, I would judge it as a reduction of the Christian message. The narrative element of worship is not on God's whole story but usually entirely on Christ paying the penalty for your sin and on your need to accept his work on your behalf.

Late Twentieth-Century Worship and the Vision of God

If you take time to study worship movements in the first half of the twentieth century, you will find that they generally follow patterns of content and style established in the seventeenth, eighteenth, and nineteenth centuries. The main focus of worship in the first half of the twentieth century kept to either an educational focus of the rationalists or the enthusiastic focus of the experientialists. Some new groups like the fundamentalists, who were the product of both the Reformed tradition coming from Princeton and the dispensational tradition, managed to embrace both traditions, not necessarily as individual churches, but as a movement. Consequently, in fundamentalist circles there are churches that keep a level of order and strong Bible teaching while other fundamentalist churches practice a more free-floating, revivalistic style of worship. There are also new late nineteenth- and early twentieth-century movements that stand in the Wesleyan holiness tradition with some slight changes. These include the Pentecostal tradition with its emphasis on tongues and the charismatic movement, known for its recovery of the gifts.

In the midforties the term *evangelical* was once again used to identify a group of churches. For the most part, evangelicals, like their fundamentalist parents, are split between the education and the experiential revivalistic models of worship.

The last half of the twentieth century saw the introduction of new models of worship based on the emergence of the contemporary chorus that sprang forth from the Jesus movement of the early seventies. At first the contemporary chorus movement was confined to the Jesus movement. But it spread to the charismatics, then to the Pentecostals, and in the last decade of the twentieth century it became prevalent in many evangelical churches as well as spawning new church movements like the Vineyard.

The contemporary chorus movement is not a theologically sensitive movement. If anything, it is *atheological.* At first, passages of Scripture, especially the Psalms, were put to music. The movement was soon influenced by the culture of narcissism, however, and the songs became more and more about *me and my worship* of God. The biblical story clarified in this book has attempted to show that worship is about God: God's wonder, mystery, and majesty; his wonderful story of rescuing his creatures and creation. The great majority of choruses, however, are about *me.* How much *I* love God and want to serve him. How *I* worship him, glorify him, magnify him, praise him, and lift him up. The focus seems to be on self-generated worship. God is made the object of *my* affection, and worship is measured by how strongly I am able to feel this gratitude and express it to God.

In recent years this *me*-orientation to worship has been brought under question by a few lone voices here and there. But for the most part the music industry has perpetuated the focus on self, and churches have not turned away from this culture-shaped content.

Contemporary worship stands in the tradition of revivalistic-enthusiastic worship, not only in its emotional value but also in its

84

order of worship. Because it is not primarily focused on God's acts of salvation from creation, incarnation, and re-creation, it does not express the narrative of God's saving action in history. Like revivalistic worship, it is more focused on the narrative that takes place in a person's heart. Therefore, the only way it really differs from its revivalistic predecessor is that it substitutes choruses for gospel songs, adds the guitar and other instruments, and has dropped the invitation. Compare, for example, the models below:

Revivalistic Model	Contemporary Model
Gospel singing (piano, organ, and choir)	**Chorus singing** (piano, guitar, drums, etc.)
Evangelistic preaching (direct from the Bible)	**Preaching** (strong emphasis on the therapeutic; gospel is not often presented)
Invitation	**Ministry/The Invitation** (has been replaced by prayer and healing ministry, especially in Pentecostal and charismatic-oriented churches; most evangelical churches have nothing after the sermon)

Seeker-oriented contemporary churches argue that worship does not need to present the whole gospel. The purpose of worship, they say, is to get people in the door. Then, after they have gained a hearing, they present the gospel in small-group settings. This argument may be good marketing, but it fails to understand the biblical purpose of worship. Worship brings glory to God because it remembers God's saving deeds in the past and anticipates God's culmination of his saving deeds in the new heavens and new earth.

Conclusion

In this chapter I have attempted to provide a bird's-eye view of the major shifts in worship over the last two thousand years. I personally realize the shortcoming of such a vast summary. A complete study of this theme would take at least a dozen PhD theses—worthy topics I might add. In spite of the largeness of the subject and the incomplete nature of my study, however, I feel that the thesis—that the fullness of God's story/vision has been lost in the West—stands.

I have made a brief comparison of the major worship trends of each paradigm of history, and what I have concluded is this:

The story of God's vision was the subject of worship in the early church.

God's story/vision was maintained in the Eastern churches.

In the medieval era the focus of God's work shifted away from the whole story to part of the story, namely his sacrifice on the cross.

During the Reformation a shift began toward the focus on self and the need for repentance, faith, and a continuous, watchful heeding of the self.

In the modern world the emphasis on worship shifted under the Enlightenment to knowledge and during the romantic era to a strong expectation of the conversion experience.

In the twentieth century, the revivalistic order continued among evangelicals but with considerable change in content, including seeker-oriented worship and a greater emphasis on therapeutic preaching.

This brief survey intends to show the need for rethinking the content of our worship.

In the postmodern world of violence and uncertainty, there is a great need to recover the *Christus Victor* theme that God in Christ has defeated all the powers of evil, that he has conclusively abolished sin, death, and all that is evil in the world, and that because of his death and resurrection, he will return for his final victory over all that is evil and set up his kingdom and reign over all the earth. The church is called to witness to this truth by its very existence and in its worship to remember these past saving events of God in history that assures the new world we anticipate.

We turn now to part 2, "Applying God's Story to Worship," where we will seek out ways to recast our worship toward the full narrative of creation, incarnation, and re-creation.

Part 2

Applying God's Story to Worship

5

Worship

Transformed by Remembrance and Anticipation

*B*ecause of my travels to various churches, worship con-ferences, and educational settings, I have met numerous people who have spoken to me about the present crisis of worship. It is a crisis in both traditional and contemporary settings. It is, you might say, a universal crisis. Traditional worship often feels dead, intellectual, and dry, whereas contemporary worship seems loud, oriented toward the self, and not very uplifting.

There are exceptions, however. I have been in traditional churches where worship is inspiring and spiritually challenging. And I have been in contemporary churches with a strong sense of the worship of almighty God. I don't think the solution is to choose one over the other. For example, I heard of the pastor of a liturgical church who said, "The problem with our worship is vestments, choir, hymns, and Eucharist. They keep people from coming to church, so we are going to get rid of all that and go contemporary." Big mistake. We need liturgical churches; we need contemporary churches. Both have a place in God's church, and both can do what I am writing about in this book.

The Crisis of Worship

While the current crisis of worship is very complex and resists a simplistic answer, I wish to offer a threefold critique that is easy to remember and that goes to the heart of the issues. I suggest that a key to the crisis is to evaluate worship through the lens of content, structure, and style.

This book is about the crisis of *content*. If worship is, as I have discussed, remembrance and anticipation, then current worship needs to be considered through these two biblical motifs.

I readily acknowledge that remembrance is a vital part of traditional hymnology and contemporary songs. Pick up an evangelical hymnbook and make your way through the hymns and songs produced by evangelical writers, and there you will find a rich treasury of sung testimony to God's wonderful works in history. The same is true of many choruses. Remembrance of God's mighty deeds is often referred to in the lyrics of traditional and contemporary songs. The problem is that God's overall work in history is ignored. His mighty deeds for world redemption are *individualized*. There is very little awareness in evangelical music that God does more than save *me*. The theme of connecting creation with incarnation that leads to re-creation is simply lacking. Therefore, even though our worship is conscious of remembrance, it is a truncated content. It does not span all of history and reach into the believer's anticipation of not only his or her salvation but of the salvation of the whole world.

The second crisis is one of *structure*. The story of God is communicated in the narrative of Word and Table. This structure is not an order of mere convenience, but an order which itself is deeply rooted in God's narrative. When the ancient structure of Word and Table is followed, worship itself narrates the worshipers' experience through remembrance and anticipation. The Word, with its readings and preaching primarily remembers God's story through the Christ event. The eucharistic prayers, songs, and symbols then usher the congregation into the anticipation of the future kingdom of God. These realities do not find *conscious* expression in evangelical worship. The basic structure of Word and Eucharist held in any church, however, is always pregnant with God's story. The story awaits its birth by the pastor and the congregation to bring the *content* of our worship in line with the biblical *order* of worship. This simple move will facilitate the recovery of remembrance and anticipation.

The third crisis is that of *style*, which is directly related to the crisis of content and structure. If it is acknowledged that the content of worship is remembrance and anticipation, it should be an easy step to take to see that the structure of worship serves the content of worship. The Word remembers and the Eucharist anticipates. (This does not mean there is no anticipation in the Word nor remembrance in the Eucharist. It is a broad generalization that stimulates provocative thought about what worship does rather than a stiff, unbending framework.) The style of doing Word and Table is a matter of making the content and structure of worship *indigenous* to the local setting. The greatest error I have seen in the style of worship—both traditional and contemporary—is to program it. Traditional worship strings together Scripture readings, prayers, psalms, choir, solo numbers, offering, and announcements and then adds the sermon and benediction at the end. Usually there is little thought given to narrating God's story and vision. On the other hand, most contemporary worship leaders think in terms of opening with thirty minutes of songs and choruses strung together, followed by a time for announcements and offering, followed by the sermon (not generally regarded as worship). The sermon is usually topical, often supplemented with a few Bible stories, but seldom about the Good News that God has won a decisive victory over the powers of evil and will eventually set up his kingdom forever. Consider what is happening in our world today with the militant terrorists who wish to cast Israel into the sea and scale the wall of the Western world and bring it to ruin. What is more relevant: a therapeutic sermon that makes you feel good about yourself, or a sermon that speaks to who narrates the world?

I find that thinking about worship in terms of content, structure, and style is a good way to organize our thoughts. Since content and structure are my primary issues, I will not spend much time with style, which is an important issue, but not as much so as the other two. Throughout history there have been numerous styles in both Eastern Orthodoxy and Roman Catholicism (although one can say that historic liturgies have evolved into fairly permanent styles) and certainly among Protestants.

We turn now to examples from ancient worship where both the content of worship and the structure of worship speak of remembrance and anticipation.

Worship in the Ancient Church

The subject of worship in the ancient church is vast and covers six hundred years. It is impossible in a book of this length to address all the complex developments, but it is possible for me to provide several examples of worship content and structure that will at least illustrate the themes of remembrance and anticipation. I will begin with the earliest description of worship from the middle of the second century, then speak to the theology of the period and provide several examples from both preaching and the eucharistic liturgy.

The Earliest Description of Worship

The earliest noncanonical description of worship appears in Justin Martyr's work *The First Apology*. Christians had been accused and actually persecuted because of a rumor that when they met to worship they sacrificed an infant and drank its blood and ate its flesh. The *Apology* was written to the emperor to explain what Christians believe and how they worship and live. It was written in AD 150 and stands today as one of the most important documents of the early church because of the insight it provides on early Christian faith and practice. Here is the description of worship:

> And on the day called Sunday, all who live in cities or in the country gather together to one place, and the memoirs of the apostles or the writings of the prophets are read, as long as time permits; then, when the reader has ceased, the president verbally instructs, and exhorts to the imitation of these good things. Then we all rise together and pray, and, as we before said, when our prayer is ended, bread and wine and water are brought, and the president in like manner offers prayers and thanksgivings, according to his ability, and the people assent, saying Amen; and there is a distribution to each, and a participation of that over which thanks have been given, and to those who are absent a portion is sent by the deacons. And they who are well to do, and willing, give what each thinks fit; and what is

collected is deposited with the president, who succours the orphans and widows, and those who, through sickness or any other cause, are in want, and those who are in bonds, and the strangers sojourning among us, and in a word takes care of all who are in need.[1]

According to Justin Martyr we may say the following things about ancient worship:

1. The public worship of the church took place on Sunday, the day of the resurrection. The *day* of worship itself is important. In the Hebrew tradition the day of worship was Saturday, the Sabbath. It is the day of God's completion of the creation and, therefore, the day to rest as God rested. ("On the seventh day he rested from all his work. And God blessed the seventh day and made it holy, because on it he rested from all the work of creating he had done," Gen. 2:2–3.) Saturday is the day of rest. But on Sunday, the first day of the week (Mark 16:2), God who rested created again. This time the resurrection reveals that Christ himself is the "new creation." In him "the old has gone, the new has come! All this is from God, who reconciled us to himself through Christ" (2 Cor. 5:17–18). The very day of worship discloses that worship is not about me enthroning God in the heavens, but about Christ who has reconciled all things to God through his death and resurrection.

2. Worship was characterized by the reading and proclamation of Scripture and the celebration of the Table. I will comment further on these two aspects of worship in chapters 6 and 7. It is sufficient at this point to state that Word and Table are not about me but about Christ, who is revealed in the Scripture and at the Table.

3. The presider "instructs, and exhorts to the imitation of these good things." We now come to the *me* aspect of worship. Here we see that worship is not that which I do, but *that which is done in me.* That is, worship, which reveals Christ, forms me by making me aware that Jesus is my spirituality and that worship is to form my spiritual life into the pattern of living into the death and resurrection of Jesus. Paul speaks to the Corinthians about this meaning of worship when he states, "Christ's love compels us, because we are convinced that one died for all, and therefore all died. And he died for all, that *those who live should no longer live for themselves but for him who died for them and was raised again*" (2 Cor. 5:14–15,

emphasis added). The purpose of worship is not that "I am the source of God's worship," but that Jesus is the one man who truly did God's service (worship) of reclaiming the world for God. So my worship, in union with Christ, is to be, as Justin states, an "imitation" of "these good things" (the disclosure of Christ in Word and Eucharist). Worship nourishes the spiritual life, then, because it discloses Christ as the one who does for me what I can't do for myself and "compels" me to doxology on my lips and to live in the pattern of death and resurrection.

4. The congregation prays.

5. Prayers and thanksgiving (Eucharist) are said over bread and wine, which are then consumed by the people present. Notice that the eucharistic prayers are said "according to his ability." The prayers at the Table now become fixed, as we will see in Hippolytus, AD 215 (discussed later in this chapter).

6. Bread and wine are sent to those who are absent.

7. A collection is taken and distributed to widows, orphans, the sick, those in prison, strangers, and all who are in need.

Justin does not give us a commentary on the theology of worship. What we do gain from his description, however, is the *structure of worship*. From the structure of Word and Table we can discern the story of God. Word and Table follow revelation and the Christ event. Broadly speaking, revelation constituted the verbal and oral presentation of God's work in history. On the other hand, the Christ event, which includes the incarnation, death, resurrection, ascension, eternal intercession on our behalf, and sure return to restore all creation and rule forever, constitutes signs that anticipate the future of God and the world. However, it must be admitted that neither Word alone nor Eucharist alone contain the full story.

Theology of the Ancient Church

Before looking at more examples of the worship of the ancient church, we should consider the dominant theology of the time. The ancient church was in a great struggle with Gnosticism—a heresy that goes all the way back to New Testament times. I have previously mentioned the Gnostics' rejection of the Old Testament, of creation, of any embrace of the physical such as an enfleshed Christ, and of any sacramental signs such as water, bread, and wine. For them, to be spiritual meant the spirit was opposed to all flesh and matter. The incarnation was not a real physical act but a spiritual *emanation* proceeding from the spirit of God to tell people the secret that would release them from their prison—the human body and earthly experience.

The battle between Orthodox Christians and the Gnostics raged around the question, "What did the apostles teach?" The Gnostics believed their faith came directly from a secret tradition held by the apostles and handed down to a few elite. The argument of the Orthodox, on the other hand, was that the Christian faith was not a secret but fully public for anyone who wished to know it. Furthermore, the Orthodox argued that the apostolic doctrine had been handed down from the apostles to their successors and that what was believed in the church was truly apostolic and dependable. (This is the origin of apostolic tradition and apostolic succession. It also accounts for the Apostles' Creed, which in its opening confession affirms, "I believe in God the Father Almighty, *maker* of heaven and earth," emphasis added.) In this battle, won by the Orthodox by the end of the second century, the church affirms the God of the Old Testament and the God of the New Testament to be one God. Creation is good. God became involved in the creation, even incarnate, to win it back to himself. Redemption, no longer the exclusive right of the soul, has now been affirmed by the consensus of the church to apply to all things created. God renews the face of the earth.

The two most prominent theologians of the late second century who fought the Gnostics and advanced the arguments that Orthodox faith was the faith of the apostles were Irenaeus and Tertullian. I will provide a few quotes from Irenaeus's *Against Heresies* (AD 180) to help us understand how this apostolic theology influenced the worship of the ancient church, but if you have time, I suggest you look at his work in full, especially book IV.

To begin, Irenaeus uses the following phrase or some version of it repeatedly in his argument against the Gnostics: "Now the church, although scattered over the whole civilized world to the end of the earth, *received from the Apostles and their disciples its faith*."[2] This particular introduction is from the "rule of faith," an early creedal statement that summarized the faith. It is noteworthy that part of the confession includes the restoration of all flesh at the end of history—a strong affirmation of the anticipation of the kingdom to come. The confession states that the church believes in "his coming from the heavens in the glory of the Father to *restore all things and to raise up all flesh*."[3]

Throughout his work, Irenaeus repeatedly draws on an incarnational theology to drive home that God saves his whole creation. God has descended in the incarnation and taken union with humanity so that humanity may ascend into union with him. This profound theme of the incarnation has rich implications for an earthed worship. By "earthed worship" I mean to emphasize how ancient worship is not an escape from this world. Worship uses the substance of nature—water, oil, bread, wine, movement, symbol—to proclaim that all of creation has been redeemed. This quote from Irenaeus captures the essential key the incarnation plays in ancient theology and worship:

> So, then, since the Lord redeemed us by his own blood, and gave his soul for our souls, and his flesh for our bodies, and poured out the Spirit of the Father to bring about the union and communion of God and man—bringing God down to men by [the working of] the Spirit, and again raising man to God by his incarnation—and by his coming firmly and truly giving us incorruption, by our communion with God, all the teachings of the heretics are destroyed. Vain are those who say that his appearance [on earth] was a mere fiction. These things did not take place fictitiously but in reality.[4]

Irenaeus goes on in the same text to develop the theology of recapitulation. This theology was first developed by the apostles in the comparison they drew between the first Adam, who brings sin, death, and condemnation, and the second Adam, who brings righteousness, life, and justification (see Rom. 5:12–21; 1 Cor. 15).

> I have shown too that to say that his appearance was only seeming is the same as to say that he took nothing from Mary. He would not have had real flesh and blood, by which he paid the price [of our salvation], unless he had indeed recapitulated in himself the ancient making of Adam. Vain therefore are the Valentinians who

teach this, and so reject the [new] life of the flesh and scorn what God has made.[5]

The recapitulation accomplished by God's Spirit is fulfilled by Jesus's death and resurrection where he wins a great victory over sin, death, and the devil. Because of this victory, which he accomplished *in the flesh*, he wins back his entire created order.

The Garden of Gethsemane reverses what happened in the Garden of Eden, and now God will rule forever in his regained garden. His world is now the place of his habitation. His glory shows forth to the ends of the earth.

> He therefore completely renewed all things, both taking up the battle against our enemy, and crushing him who at the beginning had led us captive in Adam, trampling on his head, as you find in Genesis that God said to the serpent, "And I will put enmity between you and the woman, and between your seed and her seed; he will be on the watch for your head, and you will be on the watch for his heel." From then on it was proclaimed that he who was to be born of a virgin, after the likeness of Adam, would be on the watch for the serpent's head—this is the seed of which the apostle says in the Letter to the Galatians, "The law of works was established until the seed should come to whom the promise was made." He shows this still more clearly in the same Epistle when he says, "But when the fullness of time was come, God sent his Son, made of a woman." The enemy would not have been justly conquered unless it had been a man [made] of woman who conquered him. For it was by a woman that he had power over man from the beginning, setting himself up in opposition to man. Because of this the Lord also declares himself to be the Son of Man, so renewing in himself that primal man from whom the formation [of man] by woman began, that as our race went down to death by a man who was conquered we might ascend again to life by a man who overcame; and as death won the palm of victory over us by a man, so we might by a man receive the palm of victory over death.[6]

The point of presenting the theology of the ancient church is to show that *worship does this theology*. It sings, tells, and enacts God's story, not *my* story. The primary focus of worship then and now is not me, the worshiper, but God, who redeems the world.

Worship does God's story, and God, who is the subject of worship, repeats, so to speak, his own story. God, through worship, works on me through his story to elicit praise on my lips and obedience in my living. When this happens, worship takes place.

Ancient Examples of *Remembrance* and *Anticipation*

There are numerous examples in the ancient liturgies of both re-membrance and anticipation. I will illustrate the prominence of these themes with two well-known examples, one taken from the service of the Word and another taken from the service of the Eucharist.

An Example of Remembrance *in the Ancient Service of the Word*

The first example is drawn from the earliest noncanonical sermon available. The sermon is by Melito of Sardis and was presented at the Easter Vigil around AD 195. In the Great Paschal Vigil the account of the Exodus is always read, followed by the sermon, celebrating resurrection, the new Exodus. The entire sermon is based on the typology of the Passover event with the Christ event. The sermon begins with the following words:

> The Scripture of the exodus of the Hebrews has been read,
> And the words of the mystery have been declared;
> how the sheep was sacrificed,
> and how the people was saved,
> and how the Pharaoh was flogged by the mystery.[7]

The first third of the sermon is all about the history of God loving Israel, freeing Israel from its bondage to Pharaoh, bringing them over the Red Sea, and redeeming them to be God's own people. After narrating God's provision for Israel, Melito launches into how God's saving activity with Israel is a type of the fulfillment that is to be found in Christ.

> So then, just as with the provisional examples,
> so it is with eternal things;
> as it is with things on earth,

98

so it is with the things in heaven.
For indeed the Lord's salvation and his truth were prefig-
    ured in the people,
and the decrees of the Gospel were proclaimed in advance
    by the law.

Thus the people was a type, like a preliminary sketch,
and the law was the writing of an analogy.
The Gospel is the narrative and fulfillment of the law,
and the church is the repository of reality.[8]

At this point in the sermon, Melito makes a shift in content. He returns to the Garden of Eden, to the fall, and to the subsequent involvement of God in the history of the patriarchs, setting the stage for the type of the future redemption that Israel embodies. "You have heard the narrative of the type and its correspondence: hear now the confirmation of the mystery."[9]

The mystery is the entire narrative of the Scripture that Melito aptly summarizes. He begins, "God, in the beginning" made the garden and placed man and woman in it. But they "disobeyed God" and were therefore "thrown out into the world" where "many other bizarre and most terrible and dissolute things took place among the people." Then "the Lord made advance preparation for his own suffering, in the patriarchs and in the prophets and in the whole people."[10] Thus the mystery of the Lord, prefigured from of old through the vision of type, is today fulfilled and has found faith.

Melito then moves on to the prophecies found in Moses, David, Jeremiah, and Isaiah. He concludes, "Many other things were proclaimed by many prophets concerning the mystery of the Pascha, who is Christ, to whom be the glory forever, Amen."[11]

Now Melito moves to the incarnation. He "comes as a man" to "set free the flesh from suffering." He "slew the manslayer death," he "set us free from the slavery of the devil." He "delivered us from slavery to freedom, from darkness into light, from death into life."

This is the lamb slain,
this is the speechless lamb,
this is the one born of Mary the fair ewe,
this is the one taken from the flock,

99

and led to slaughter.
Who was sacrificed in the evening,
and buried at night;
who was not broken on the tree,
who was not undone in the earth,
who rose from the dead and resurrected humankind from
   the grave below.[12]

As Melito moves toward the end of the sermon, he ties all things from the beginning to the end to show that Christ is the very center of the universe, that all history and the kingdom to come is interpreted through him:

He it is who made the heaven and the earth,
and formed humanity in the beginning,
who was proclaimed through the law and the prophets,
who took flesh from a virgin,
who was hung on a tree,
who was buried in earth,
who was raised from the dead,
and ascended to the heights of heaven,
who sits at the right hand of the father,
who has the power to save all things,
through whom the father acted from the beginning and for
   ever.[13]

The translator of Melito's *On Pascha* provides his own introduction to the work. His concluding comments are instructive for us because he reflects the presence of remembrance and anticipation in Melito's work.

On Pascha is a liturgical document, and in the light of the Jewish understanding of remembrance as a means of making the past a present reality, and bringing to bear the blessings of the past in the hope of the future, we may understand that for Melito and for his hearers the liturgy was the point at which the glory of God in Jesus Christ, the resurrection triumph and the pains of the passion, the mysteries proclaimed by the Scriptures and the experience of salvation now and in the future came to life and reality.[14]

100

Clearly the reading of Scriptures and preaching is a remembrance of God's mighty saving deeds as well as an expectation of his final triumph over all evil; God's past deeds *anticipate* God's future. For Melito worship does God's story.

An Example of Anticipation in the Ancient Service of the Eucharist

To illustrate remembrance and anticipation in the ancient church, I will draw from the earliest example of the eucharistic prayer. This prayer recorded by Hippolytus of Rome about AD 215 presents the common structure and content of eucharistic prayers everywhere. There are many variations of it, but *On the Apostolic Tradition* is believed by liturgical scholars to be the sourcebook for both Eastern and Western liturgies prayed in the third century and beyond.[15]

According to Hippolytus, the essence of the prayers goes as far back as Justin Martyr (AD 150). He writes that as a young boy he heard the content of the prayer he now writes down. According to Justin, as mentioned before, the presider "offers prayers and thanksgivings, *according to his ability*" (emphasis added). This phrase suggests that the prayer in its earliest stages of development was spontaneous. Hippolytus now claims he is putting the prayer into writing to serve as a guideline for pastors. There seems to be no intention that the prayer always be said with the same words but that the structure and truth of the prayer be preserved as it is handed down from generation to generation of pastors. It was much later that the eucharistic prayer became standardized in various Christian centers. Here is the prayer recorded by Hippolytus with my commentary on the side.

The Text of Hippolytus

Order	Text	Commentary
Dominus vobiscum	The Lord be with you *And all shall say:* And with your spirit.	
Sursum Corda	Up with your hearts. We have (them) with the Lord. . . . It is fitting and right.	Worship ascends into heaven around the throne of God.

Order	Text	Commentary
Preface Prayer	We render thanks to you O God, through your beloved child Jesus Christ, whom in the last times you sent to us as savior and redeemer and angel of your will; . . .	The preface to the prayer of thanksgiving is a proclamation.
Sanctus	[Not found in Hippolytus.]	In the Sanctus, the church joins with the angels and archangels in heavenly song.
Prayer of Thanksgiving	. . . who is your inseparable Word, through whom you made all things, and in whom you are well pleased. You sent him from heaven into a virgin's womb; and conceived in the womb, he was made flesh and was manifested as your Son, being born of the Holy Spirit and the Virgin. Fulfilling your will and gaining for you a holy people, he stretched out his hands when he should suffer, that he might release from suffering those who have believed in you. And when he was betrayed to voluntary suffering that he might destroy death, and break the bonds of the devil, and tread down hell, and shine upon the righteous, and fix a term, and manifest the resurrection, . . .	The prayer of thanksgiving is a recall of God's mighty acts in history, particularly God's act of salvation in Jesus Christ. Note the creedal nature of the prayer as it recounts creation, incarnation, death, resurrection, overthrow of evil, and establishment of the church.
Words of Institution	. . . he took bread and gave thanks to you saying, "Take, eat, this is my body which shall be broken for you." Likewise also the cup saying, "This is my blood, which is shed for you; when you do this you make my remembrance."	The repetition of the words of Jesus lie at the heart of the Table action.
Anamnesis	Remembering therefore his death and resurrection, we offer to you the bread and the cup, giving you thanks because you have held us worthy to stand before you and minister to you.	The word *anamnēsis* means "recall" and refers not to a mental memory but a divine action in which Christ, the head of the church, is remembered with the body.
Offering		This is the offering of the church's praise, which ministers to God.

102

Order	Text	Commentary
Epiclesis	And we ask that you send your Holy Spirit upon the offering of your holy Church; that, gathering her into one, you would grant to all who receive the holy things (to receive) for the fullness of the Holy Spirit for the strengthening of faith in truth; . . .	The Holy Spirit is invoked so that those who partake may be confirmed in truth by the work of the Spirit.
Closing Doxology	. . . that we may praise and glorify you through your child Jesus Christ, through whom be glory and honor to you, to the Father and the Son, with the Holy Spirit, in your holy Church, both now and to the ages of ages. Amen[16]	The prayer ends with a trinitarian doxology

First, note the structure of the prayer. It is organized around the Triune God. The Trinity is not presented as an abstract concept—a God who sits in the heavens simply named Father, Son, and Spirit. No, God is the God who dwells in the heavens yet is active here on earth winning his world back to himself by defeating the powers of sin and death.

Second, note the content of each of the three main parts of the prayer. The prayer begins in the heavens with a preface prayer and the *Sanctus* (not in Hippolytus but in nearly all the extant prayers of the third century). In the ancient church, the early Fathers, drawing on the book of Revelation (the worship book of the ancient church), regarded the earthly church as ascending into the heavens in the eucharistic prayer to offer thanks to God together with the angels, the archangels, and the whole heavenly host.

The prayer then moves to the reason why the church offers its thanksgiving. Here in the prayer of thanksgiving we encounter both remembrance and anticipation. The prayer is cryptic. However, it manages to tie together creation, incarnation, and re-creation. It focuses on *Christus Victor*—on the deliverance that Christ brings because he has destroyed death, broken the bonds of the devil, and tread down hell. Because he has accomplished this mission of his Father, he has "opened the windows of heaven" (a phrase frequently used in the liturgy) and made possible the restoration of the entire

103

created order. The narrative section then ends with the words of institution.

Finally, the prayer turns to the Holy Spirit. The Holy Spirit is asked to do his work, that God send the Spirit upon the church, making it one. And the Spirit is asked to bless the offering of bread and wine that those who receive it may experience a confirmation of the truth to which the bread and wine witness.

What we have seen in these two examples taken from the primary structure and content of ancient Christian worship is that worship breathed remembrance and anticipation. Both themes are rooted firmly in Jewish worship and continued in the worship of the church. Herein lies the key to biblical worship. What should we do with it?

Application of *Remembrance* and *Anticipation* to an Ancient-Future Worship

I have emphasized throughout this book how worship does God's story or vision. There is another way to state this: *worship does truth*.

The ancient church captured how worship does truth in the phrase *lex orandi; lex credendi; est.* Strictly translated this phrase means, "The rule of prayer is the rule of faith." Another way to state the essence of this Latin phrase is to say, "Show me how you worship and I'll show you what you believe." If *how* we worship shapes *what* we believe, then it is imperative that we pay attention to how we worship. If worship is shaped by culture, it will result in a culturally conditioned faith. If worship is shaped by narcissism, it will result in a *me*-oriented consumer faith. So how do we go about breaking culture-bound worship and return worship to the story of God that shapes us into the image of Christ? I have already mentioned two clues from early Christian worship. The first is to recover the order of worship; the second is to recover the content of worship.

Recover the Ancient Order of Worship

First, the order of worship itself has something to do with how worship reveals the truth about Jesus. I challenge every pastor, music minister, and worship leader to look at how worship is currently ordered in your church and ask, "What does the order of worship actually communicate? How does it inform our faith and shape our spiritual life?"

If your structure of worship is oriented toward a "program" for an "audience," then what do these words *program* and *audience* say about your worship? They say worship is a presentation. This view of worship arises out of the shift from print to broadcast communication. Although television was introduced in the forties and fifties, it wasn't until the sixties that the media revolution really began to impact culture and worship. By the seventies and eighties, program design had become a science. Worship followed the curvature of culture, and worship leaders became program designers. Some worship leaders have ignored content in favor of technical programming. I have spoken in conferences where the worship has been designed to the minute. The program coordinator sits me down at some point before the "event" (now called "gathering") to walk through the service. The program design usually reads like this:

> We begin at 10:00 a.m. sharp with a set of songs that take us to 10:18. From 10:18 to 10:20 we have a prayer and welcome. Announcements will be given from 10:20 to 10:24. There will be another set of songs from 10:24 to 10:30. Between 10:30 and 10:38 there will be a skit. You will preach from 10:38 to 11:23. After the sermon there will be another set of songs until 11:29. Then, give an ending prayer at 11:29 to 11:30. Got it?
> Yep . . .
> That's the program. Let's pray for God's blessing.

Actually, this illustration is only a metaphor of what a "timing of worship" design looks like. Usually the various "acts" of worship are timed to the second and resemble a complex TV show.

In this worship the end is often driven by a desire to please the audience. Questions asked may include:

Did you enjoy the worship today?

Did it move fast enough to keep your attention?

How was the skit; did it properly set up the sermon?

Did any of our performers go overtime?

How can we make our next service more engaging?

Unfortunately, the audience demand for "Let's never do it the same way twice," or, "What I love about this worship is that you never know what's going to happen," will ultimately drain the leaders physically, emotionally, and spiritually.

One worship leader told me how much his church loved doing creative worship. "Give me an example," I responded.

"Well, last week we began with the benediction and ended with the call to worship."

"Well that was quite different!" I said as I tried to contain my shock.

Anyone who travels and visits churches will see that *program, theme,* and *creative* are the most dominant words of worship planning that force leaders toward designing culturally driven worship. My concern is that culturally driven worship will nurture a culturally formed spiritual life. If this is true, how do we correct current worship practices so that it does truth and forms the congregation into a deeper, more biblically informed spirituality? I suggest we look once again at the ancient order of worship and ask how it shapes the spiritual life.

The ancient order of worship was Word and Table. Worship is ordered by revelation and incarnation. God is first disclosed to the world through revelation. Then God becomes incarnate in the world in Jesus Christ, who accomplishes our salvation. This order of revelation-incarnation is not coincidental; it is fundamental to the outworking of God's story. God's story is proclaimed in Word and Table. We *hear* God's story; we *see* God's story. This structure is revealed in the first description of worship in Acts 2:42, where they gathered around "the apostles' teaching" and "the breaking of the bread" in the context of fellowship and prayer. This structure of Word and Table orders another ancient description of worship—the experience of Cleopas and his companion on the road to Emmaus (Luke 24). First they heard the story when Jesus "explained to them what was said in all the Scriptures concerning himself" (Luke 24:27), and second, "When he was at the table with them, he took bread, gave thanks, broke it and began to give it to them. Then their eyes

106

were opened and they recognized him" (Luke 24:30–31). There is a way to tell and enact the story of God, and it is in the double service of the Word and Table. For here, in the very order of worship, God's story, the substance of our worship, is disclosed and God is seen in his glory.

Recover the Ancient Content of Worship

Second, the order of worship reveals the *content* of worship. This is a simple way to describe biblical worship, but let's unpack the richness and depth to which these few words point. The central focus of worship is God's story, not my story or a particular nation's story, but God's relationship to all creatures and creation. The story encompasses all of human existence and all world history from creation to re-creation.

The two words used throughout this book to point to *how* God's story relates to worship are *remembered* and *anticipated*. These are the two central acts of biblical and historical worship. The story is *remembered* through Scripture reading and preaching; the story is *anticipated* through the Table. The story is also the very substance of our singing, praying, and testimonies. It shapes our environment, determines how the arts are employed, and informs everything else we do. And, though God is the subject of worship, acting among the people, it is the *people* of God who remember God's story, not as an audience, but as true participants in the very story that tells the truth about the world and all of human existence. The two sides of this substance in worship are the content, which is God's story, and the energy with which God's story is remembered and anticipated by the people.

There is a picture that captures the divine and human substance of worship; it is Michelangelo's depiction of God reaching out to man and man reaching out to God, the fingers of both nearly touching. The two fingers say it is God who first initiates a relationship with us, but man must respond. Worship is the story between the two fingers. It is the story of how God and man, once united in the garden but now separated by the fall, express their union. But the man whose finger is stretched forth to touch the finger of God is not everyman. It is, so to speak, the finger of the one man, who

107

for all mankind reestablished the union between man and God, and his name is Jesus.

The biblical teaching that Jesus is our worship dispels all notions of self-generated worship. We are fallen creatures whose union with God has been shattered, twisted, broken, even severed. We have rebelled against God, gone in a direction away from God, inverted to the self, proclaiming salvation through self-actualization. Our fingers do not reach toward God but toward the self, whom we worship and adore as the God of the universe, the one around whom all things revolve. The whole story of God is about Jesus, God incarnate, who became man that we might be united to God.

Worship discloses the work of Jesus Christ. He himself is the eternal *leiturgia* (liturgy) of God. (The word *liturgy* is a common Greek word that refers to your work or occupation. Carpenters, doctors, lawyers each have their own work or liturgy.) The work of Christ now continues in the heavens where he is doing the work of eternal intercession. He is the one man who has served God and through his service has won creatures and creation back to God. He fulfills and replaces all the rituals of the tabernacle and temple that pointed to him. He is the new Adam, the new covenant, the new circumcision, the new Sabbath rest, the new Paschal Lamb. He is the one in whom "God was pleased to have all his fullness dwell" so that "through him" he might "reconcile to himself all things, whether things on earth or things in heaven, by making peace through his blood, shed on the cross" (Col. 1:19–20). And we have "been buried with him in baptism and raised with him through your faith in the power of God, who raised him from the dead" (Col. 2:12).

Jesus Christ does for us what we cannot do for ourselves. As God incarnate, he is our obedience, he is our faith, he is our new life, and he is our eternal intercession before the Father. What was lost in Adam has been restored in Jesus Christ. God *became* the second Adam to reverse the failure of the first Adam. So God, who created, became incarnate so that he might re-create and win back his creation and creatures from the power that rebelled against him. And in the end of history, the second Adam will finally crush the powers of evil, defeating their presence and power in the world forever. So what then is the worship that the people of God do? We

108

remember God's saving deeds and anticipate his vision, his final rule over all creation.

Nourished by an Ancient-Future Worship through a Passion for Truth

Ancient worship, then, does truth. All one has to do is to study the ancient liturgies to see that liturgies clearly do truth by their order and in their substance. This is why so many young people today are now adding ancient elements to their worship.

In almost every evangelical college and seminary in North America, students who have been put off by culturally driven, programmed worship are experimenting with ancient worship. They do worship that follows the order of Word and Table. They have introduced more Scripture reading, more interactive prayer litanies, more ancient hymns, more time for silence, and the passing of the peace. Worship is almost always eucharistic. People come forward to receive the Eucharist, singing the great hymns of the church interspersed with relational songs as they receive bread and wine. And usually the anointing with oil with the laying on of hands and prayers for healing are conducted along with the reception of bread and wine. There is also a great deal of concern to create an environment of reverence, quiet, and centering prayer so that the meaning of God's story is received in contemplation. This recovery of ancient practices is not the mere restoration of ritual but a deep, profound, and passionate engagement with truth—truth that forms and shapes the spiritual life into a Christlikeness that issues forth in the call to a godly and holy life and into a deep commitment to justice and to the needs of the poor.

The motivation of these younger evangelicals is not that of rebellion against the culturally formed, programmed worship of their parents' generation but a genuine and authentic recovery of truth embraced with a passionate desire to be a real disciple of Jesus, a person formed in the image of Christ. What these young people have rediscovered is that worship nourishes their spiritual identity and feeds their commitment to fulfill the spiritual life in a deeply committed way.

Conclusion

I began this chapter by pointing to the crisis of structure and content in Protestant worship. I have, throughout the text, woven the pattern of Word and Table with the biblical emphasis on the remembrance of God's mighty acts of salvation and the anticipation of the final vision of God in a restored world.

There is much more that can be said about how worship does God's story and vision, but space does not permit any more examples. Let it be said, though, that all aspects of worship—confession of sins, preaching, praying, passing the peace, silence, the Eucharist, and then special services of worship in the Christian year or particular services of marriage, ordination, and even funerals—ultimately proceed from God's story as their source and have the power to form our spirituality.

One way to worship personally is to simply delight in the story that worship does. The delight of worship is not:

"That was a great program!"

"I loved the music today."

"What an entertaining sermon."

"I really felt like I was worshiping today."

"That sure was fun dancing around, shouting 'Amen!' and giving my neighbor a high five."

These descriptions ultimately are a delight in self as if "I did it; I broke through; I really worshiped." Worship that generates that kind of response is not worship. True worship generates the sense of:

"What a great story!"

"I can't believe that God would do that for the world and for me."

"What a God to become human and to restore all things through Christ."

For some people the truth declared in worship will be received with exuberance; for others the truth of God's story will be received with reserve, a quiet sense of joy, or even relief. But with us all, a worship that does God's story should result in a delight that produces participation.

Because God is the subject who acts upon me in worship, my participation is not reduced to verbal responses or to singing, but it is living in the pattern of the one who is revealed in worship. God, as the subject of worship, acts through the truth of Christ remembered and envisioned in worship. This truth forms me by the Spirit of God to live out the union I have with Jesus by calling me to die to sin and to live in the resurrection.

6

Word

Transformed by the Narrative Nature of Scripture

We are nourished in worship by Jesus Christ, who is the living Word disclosed to us in the Scriptures, the written Word of God. In spite of all the emphasis we evangelicals have placed on the importance of the Bible, there seems to be a crisis of the Word among us. Consider what two evangelical pastors have to say.

Pastor Jason Snook comments, "How ironic that Protestantism in particular, has moved so far away from an emphasis on the Word from which it found its origin!"[1] Pastor Dave Wiebe thinks we are in a time of "closing the book." He believes that "more and more people are choosing to endorse and follow beliefs that are not in the book or not based on the book; they are cultural and societal myths."[2] If these comments are indicative of what is taking place in our worship, then there is clearly a need to rethink our approach to Scripture in worship.

The Crisis of the Word

One crisis of Scripture is that we stand over the Bible and read God's narrative from the outside instead of standing within the narrative and reading Scripture as an insider. Two prominent ways of "outside reading" include reading the Bible through historical and literary criticism of the text or, approaching the Bible in an opposite way, reading the Bible for "what it says to me." The former is thoroughly objective, the latter, completely subjective. Neither of these "outside" forms reads Scripture in its narrative nature, nor do they adequately disclose the vision of God's reign over all creation.

Reading the Bible through Historical and Literary Criticism

The modern rise of reason and science as the philosophical universal through which everything is interpreted has wrongly impacted the way we approach Scripture. The story of how reason and science were applied to the biblical text is far too complicated to tell in any kind of detail here. Let it be sufficient to say that the Bible was read differently after the advent of historical and literary criticism in the eighteenth century than it was in the Reformation or before.

Scholars who applied historical criticism to Scripture raised serious questions about the historical accuracy of the Bible. They asked:

Are the events in the Bible real historical events?
Does the creation story describe an event that actually happened in history?
Was there really a flood?
Were Abraham and Moses real historical figures?
Is the Exodus event an actual occurrence in history?

These questions were not only applied to the Old Testament, they were also asked of the New Testament. Questions were even raised about the historicity of Jesus in a movement known as "The Quest for the Historical Jesus." These questions of historical verifiability continue in certain circles to this very day, especially in the famous Jesus Seminar, where liberal scholars seek to determine which of the sayings attributed to Jesus in the Bible were actually said by him.

114

Another group of scholars, the literary critics, approached the Bible with a different set of questions. They wanted to know how the books of the Bible came into being. Previously it was believed that if a book bore the name of a particular author, then, of course, that author and no other penned the book. But literary criticism looked at the Old Testament in particular as originating out of various communities, reflecting particular insights of those communities. Finally, it was argued, a redactor took those various stories and wove them together into the Bible we have today. Literary criticism claimed to be able to identify the various styles of writing and thus uncover the schools of thought and the varying communities that gave rise to the different strands of the Old Testament literature. Similar approaches were taken to the New Testament writing suggesting, for example, that books attributed to Paul were written by people in the school of Paul rather than by Paul himself. The underlying motif of both historical and literary criticism is that the Bible is the product of humanity, a human search for God, not a revelation from God himself.

So how did historical and literary ways of reading the Bible affect the way the Bible was read and preached? A new way of reading the Bible was introduced into both the liberal and conservative Christian camps. Conservatives read the Bible not so much to find out what it had to say but to prove its historic and scientific accuracy and to defend the authorship of the various books of the Bible. Because the liberal critics taught that the Bible was not historically or scientifically correct, the conservatives rightly saw that the truth of the Bible as a revelation from God was at stake. The conservative argument against the liberals focused on the conviction that God could not lie, and since God does not lie, the Bible must be accurate in everything it says about history and science. So conservatives read the Bible defensively.

The original meaning of the biblical narrative became lost as conservatives rushed to verify the Bible as a historical and scientific document. For example, the purpose of the creation narratives shifted from God's liturgy and a vision for the world and its people to a historical and scientific account of the beginnings of the world. The historical and scientific way of reading the Bible distanced the readers from the "who of the Bible" to the "when and how of creation."

115

Advocates of the historical or scientific approach to the Bible began to fight over the seven-day theory of creation, the concept of a young earth, the validity of a particular date for the Exodus event. Evidence for the historicity of Christ became the *real* issues of Bible study. This apologetic and defensive style of reading made its way into the pulpit by earnest defenders of the Bible. The vision of God's intended relationship with creature and creation was forsaken as the issue of "proving the Bible to be true" became primary. In the meantime the narrative nature of the Bible and God's story of all history became lost.

For example, my seminary education focused largely on the historical and literary issues. Can this account be verified by reason, science, or archaeology? Was this passage written by the person who claimed to write it, or did someone else pen these words? I soon found myself caught up in these questions. They had a way of drawing me into their orbit. I found the academic approach to the Bible to be stimulating and provocative. It promoted interesting discussions and debates, but after a while I found myself asking more crucial questions: What does this passage mean? What should I hear? What is its message? How do I interpret this passage for my spiritual life? What does it say to the average congregation about their life in the world? I soon realized that my seminary education, with its emphasis on reading the Bible historically and scientifically, was inadequate. I was trained to defend the accuracy of Scripture, but I really did not know in any kind of depth what it had to say to me, to my students, or to the local congregation.

My liberal friends were not any better off; they also bought into the historical and literary method. But, unlike the conservatives who felt they had to prove the Bible against its critics, the liberals set about to reinterpret the Bible through myth. The accounts of the Bible, they said, are stories that originated out of a religious truth. They were told and retold and gradually developed into the form in which they now appear. The interpreter's task, said the liberal, was to demythologize the stories to find the kernel truth that they represent. For example, I visited a college friend who was a student in a liberal seminary. He told me with a great deal of enthusiasm how the liberal view of Scripture functioned. He said,

Take, for example, the story that Jesus walked on the water. Obviously, Jesus didn't really walk on water. This story probably originated on the shores of Galilee. Followers of Jesus were reflecting on his ministry. Perhaps someone said, "Yeah, he was so great, he could have walked on water." From this innocent beginning the story grew into an account of Jesus walking on the water. The truth of this story is not that he walked on water but the wonder and awe in which his disciples held him. The value, then, of the walking on water story for us is that it provokes within us the feelings of awe and wonder toward Jesus.

Like the rational defense of the Bible, however, the liberal reading of myth held no power for its readers and hearers. The Bible could not claim any uniqueness. If the Scripture was reduced to a myth to provoke the idea of the sacred, how was it any different from the Greek myths or the myths and stories of other religions?

Conservatives and liberals found themselves at the same dead-end street. The Scriptures became dead for both. One lost interest in the Bible through the defense of Scripture, the other through the mythological view of the Bible. The dead-end street was named "loss of meaning." People were not nourished by the "I can prove the Bible to be true" mentality, nor was there any sustenance in the viewpoint that it is "a great myth full of wisdom." Many pastors, like myself, lost interest in historical criticism and scientific proof and turned away from this way of reading the Bible. Instead of rediscovering the narrative, many became influenced by inspirational, motivational, and therapeutic models of preaching. These models were not dependent on biblical knowledge. The tragic result of the shift into therapeutic preaching is that the study of the biblical text and its story line and vision became neglected by pastor and people.

Experiential Reading of the Bible

Another school of evangelicals were influenced by a strong anti-intellectual attitude toward Scripture. They were the experientialists, who said, "Read the Bible for what it says to you." This school of thought is found in many churches heavily influenced by revivalism and experiential small groups. Bible reading might look like this: a group gathers in a home or a church and reads a Scripture asking,

117

"What does it say to you?" The positive aspect of this approach is that the Bible is seen, not as the product of the human imagination, but as the revelation from God. So God does speak through the Bible. The negative aspect of this way of reading Scripture is that imagination runs wild. People hear what they want to hear, and often they become very dogmatic about what they think they have heard. Also, and perhaps even more egregious, are claims to a special revelation from God. There are times when groups set aside the teaching of Scripture to focus on a "message from God" given to a leader in their midst. While the significance of a personal message from God may result in a sense of immediacy, it is problematic in the long run because it considers the historic revelation of God to be of less value than the most recent personal insight or alleged new revelation. So the Bible, as valued as people proclaim it to be with their lips, is not quite as nourishing for day-to-day living. Consequently, the Bible is devalued.

Other experiential approaches to reading the Bible include turning the Bible into a therapeutic book: reading it as a book that teaches successful principles for living, reading it as guidelines for the development of personal relationships, or reading it as a book of divine business principles. I don't doubt that all these insights might be mined from the Bible, but somehow all these approaches to the Bible—the historical, scientific, mythological, experiential, and therapeutic, as well as others I have mentioned—all seem to stand *over* the Bible and ask, "What do *I* see in the Bible?" So the crisis of the Bible in our modern age is a crisis of our own making. We have put ourselves *over* the Bible, making ourselves the interpreters of the Bible, looking in the Bible for what we want to see to satisfy the primary issue *we* take to the Bible, whether history, science, myth, experience, therapy, or principles for successful living and work. If this is not the way to read or preach the Bible, we need to ask how then should the Bible be read? Let's put this question to the ancient church fathers.

Reading and Preaching the Word in the Ancient Church

The modern way of reading the Bible, which I have described above, never nourished my spiritual life. I have frequently talked to students who have lost interest in reading the Bible after taking courses on the historical and literary criticism of the Bible. I have also conversed with those who have read the Bible looking for answers to their needs, such as therapy, business principles, or some such motivating factor. These people tell me the search for these principles generated a lot of interest at first. But then they lost interest in reading the Bible once their particular curiosity had been met.

So how do you read the Bible so that it nourishes the spiritual life with its unending depth? I have found that the way of the ancient fathers brings a person inside Scripture and continually feeds the spiritual life from within the story of God. Because the ancient fathers' way of reading Scripture is also the apostolic way, we begin our search to be nourished by reading the Bible with the apostles.

The Apostles' Way of Reading and Preaching Scripture

The apostolic way of reading and preaching Scripture is to see Jesus Christ as the subject of the entire Bible, the subject of all history. He is the single overarching story of all time. He is the meaning of the entire narrative of human history. He is seen everywhere. He is in every event such as creation and the Exodus; he is in every person such as Moses or David; he is in every worship institution such as the tabernacle, the temple, the Sabbath, or the Passover. He is "the Alpha and the Omega" (Rev. 1:8), the beginning and the end. He is the Messiah, the fulfillment of Israel (Acts 2:36). He is the "image of the invisible God" (Col. 1:15). "God was pleased to have all his fullness dwell in him" (Col. 1:19). He is the "firstborn over all creation . . . by him all things were created" (Col. 1:15–16). "He is before all things, and in him all things hold together" (Col. 1:17). It is through him that God was pleased "to reconcile to himself all things, whether things on earth or things in heaven, by making peace through his blood, shed on the cross" (Col. 1:20).

When I present this "Christ is everywhere in the Bible" hermeneutic to some of my pastor friends, the idea is sometimes treated with doubt, sometimes greeted with astonishment ("I've never heard that before"), but always tested with, "Where do you get that?" The answer is Jesus himself. On the road to Emmaus Jesus responds to the despair of Cleopas and his companion by pointing to the *Jesus hermeneutic* of Scripture. "'How foolish you are, and slow of heart to believe all that the prophets have spoken! Did not the Christ have to suffer these things and then enter his glory?' And beginning with Moses and all the Prophets, he explained to them what was said in *all the Scriptures concerning himself*" (Luke 24:25–27, emphasis added). The New Testament writers as well as the fathers of the church saw the entire story of God from Genesis through Revelation, from creation to re-creation through the incarnation, death, and resurrection of Jesus Christ. Thus the Bible nourishes us not because we can prove it, not because it is the great myth of the universe, not because it stimulates interesting private experiences, but because it reveals Jesus Christ, the second Adam, who reconciles all things to God (Col. 1:20), who now lives in us and calls us into the new humanity.

To proclaim Jesus Christ as the beginning, the center, and the end of all creation and all history is not subject to intellectual analysis or historical verification, nor is it determined by any human argument or apologetic defense. It is only realized out of an act of submissive faith that steps into the story crying, "I believe, help my unbelief." We surrender our entire self—our mind, our heart, our soul, our will, our bodies—to this Christ. He lives in us as Paul said, "Christ lives in me" (Gal. 2:20).

Paul himself did not understand how Christ was all in all, how Christ was present in Jewish history, how Christ was the fulfillment of all history past, how Christ was for the Gentile and the whole world, how Christ now dwells within us. But Paul knew how to submit himself to the truth of Christ's completeness and "everywhereness." In a moment of incredible doxological praise, Paul gives us the key to seeing Christ everywhere. After having declared that "neither height nor depth, nor anything else in all creation, will be able to separate us from the love of God that is in Christ Jesus our Lord" (Rom. 8:39), he launches into an attempt in Romans 9–11 to understand God's love for the Hebrew people, the fulfillment in Jesus, and now the inclusion of the Gentiles in his giving of himself for the whole world. In the end, Paul can't figure it out. Instead he simply embraces it and bursts into the praise of God whose ways he affirms without fully grasping.

120

> Oh, the depth of riches of the wisdom and knowledge of
>   God!
> How unsearchable his judgments,
>   and his paths beyond tracing out!
> "Who has known the mind of the Lord?
>   Or who has been his counselor?"
> "Who has ever given to God,
>   that God should repay him?"
> For from him and through him and to him are all things.
>   To him be the glory forever! Amen.
>
> Romans 11:33–36

The centrality of Christ to all of history and to the meaning of human existence invites us into Jesus Christ, through whom we read the entire Bible from beginning to end. As pastors of the Word, there is a strong need to soak ourselves in the Triune story of God with its detailed exposition of the central role of Christ in the greatest drama of human history—*the drama of God who becomes one of us to rescue the world.* This theme of God's rescue of us all—not inspirational topics, motivational speakers, or massive therapy sermons—needs to be recovered as the central message of our church. This is not only the apostles' way of reading and preaching the Scripture, it is also the way of the ancient fathers and, for the most part, the churches that do an ancient-future worship.

The Ancient Fathers' Way of Reading and Preaching Scripture

Irenaeus, the most influential church father of the second century, sets forth the centrality of Christ to God's story in his work, *On the Apostolic Preaching.* In a recent translation by John Behr, Behr writes in the introduction, "Irenaeus does not present Christianity, in the way we have come to think of it, as a system of theological beliefs." Rather, Behr points out that "Irenaeus follows the example of the great speeches in Acts, recounting all the various deeds of God culminating in the exaltation of His crucified Son, our Lord Jesus Christ, and the bestowal of His Holy Spirit and the gift of a new heart of flesh."[3] Irenaeus, like Ignatius, bishop of Antioch (AD 110), and like Justin Martyr (AD 150), who preceded him, follows

121

the Christocentric reading of Scripture. The Old Testament foreshadows Jesus, who fulfills all the typologies of the Old Testament. Irenaeus reads the entire Scripture as the story of God. It is the story of how God rescues and redeems a fallen creation through Jesus Christ by the power of the Spirit.

This method of interpretation, used by the early fathers, was known as a *figural* reading of the Scripture. During the Enlightenment, figural reading was dismissed and disregarded. But the collapse of the search for the authorial intent and the unfavorable reaction against the relativism of the reader-response theory has led many to return once again to the figural reading of Scripture.

A figural reading of Scripture will read the Scripture as a whole. It will connect events and persons of the Hebrew Scripture with the events and persons of the New Testament in a rich and compelling way that will draw on the imagination. The major figures include:

Jesus is the new Adam (Romans 5:12–21).

Jesus is the new Melchizedek (Hebrews 7).

Jesus is the new Moses (John 3:14).

Jesus is the new Joshua (Hebrews 4:1–13).

Jesus is the new David (John 7:40–42).

Jesus is like Jonah (Matthew 12:39–41).

Jesus is also the new Exodus (1 Corinthians 10:1–13).

Jesus is the new tabernacle, the new high priest who completes the final sacrifice and now intercedes for us in the heavenly tabernacle (Hebrews 7–10).

Jesus is the new Passover Lamb (1 Corinthians 5:7).

Jesus is the new Sabbath (Hebrews 4:9–11).

The narrative of the whole Scripture is about Jesus Christ. We find him everywhere and in everything. To find Christ in all of Scripture is a very old, yet a very new way to read the Bible.

While the early church fathers are Christ-centered in their reading of Scripture, they do not neglect the Father and the Spirit. The life of the Son is in the communal life of the Father and the Spirit.

The Father sends the Son to redeem, to rescue the world from the clutches of the evil one. The Spirit is the one who breathes life into the world and gives life to all the events and persons who prefigure Christ. He is present in all the events of the Old Testament, as well as the ministry and work of Jesus. He is now present in the church and in God's people providing us with a conscious and intentional life of Christ to all who live in his name. When we are baptized into the death and resurrection of Jesus, the Holy Spirit is the one who gives us the new life in Christ. In this way we are brought up in the life of God's community where we fellowship in the love of the Father, Son, and Spirit.

So the fathers of the church, while Christocentric in their reading and preaching of the Scripture, were also trinitarian. For the Father is a sending God. He sends the Son; he sends the Spirit. Through them (God's two hands), the work of reclaiming the world is accomplished. Thus, to read and preach the Scripture Christocentrically, one must always say "the Father is sovereign" and "the Spirit is the life-giving and empowering reality to all that is prefigured and to all that is fulfilled by the Son."

Application: Reading and Preaching the Bible Today

The modern way of reading and preaching the Scripture has proven to be problematic. We moderns have stood over the New Testament texts with our historical, literary, and linguistic tools, picking away the brush to uncover the one single meaning the author intended to convey.

Perhaps we have limited our search to find the author's intent because we fear the more experiential and postmodern approach to texts called "reader-response theory." This theory disregards the author's intent and argues that the meaning of the text is the meaning the reader takes away from it. This highly subjective approach to reading is the other side of the pendulum to the modern problem of privileging reason and science. If a text means whatever a reader thinks it means, it has no real meaning.

So here we are in a postmodern world, stuck between two dead ends. Is there a pathway out of the road that will lead us away from extreme objectivism on the one hand and from extreme subjectivism on the other hand?

There is, but to find this path we must reverse the Enlightenment approach of our reading. Instead of using our hermeneutical tools to verify the Bible, interpret the Bible, or cull from it the principles of living, we need to step into the Bible, put ourselves within the Scripture, and allow *it* to interpret all of life including our daily living and world history. But how do we stand inside the Scripture and let it interpret the whole world including our personal life here and now?

We must read and preach the Bible as true. To do that we must turn away from a dependence on historical or scientific verification of the Bible as true. The Bible stands on its own as an interpretation of the world and is self-verified by its internal structure and content.

A few years ago I was discussing the crisis of the Bible in a graduate class I taught at Wheaton College. I spoke against reading the Bible to prove it, or reading it as a myth, or reading it through the eye of therapy, business, or personal success. One of my students, a mature woman, began to cry. "I don't know how to read the Bible," she said. "Those are the only alternatives I've ever heard. Tell me," she pleaded, "how should I read the Bible?"

I answered, "Read it as true."

Notice I did not say "read it as *if* it were true." That would be to read it mythologically. I also did not say, "Read it and *make* it true." That would be to read it to prove it. Nor did I say, "Read it *for truths*." That kind of reading usually looks for principles to make life more successful. So what are the steps we must take to read the Bible as true so that it remembers God's saving activity in history and anticipates God's reign over all creation?

1. Read and Preach the Bible with an Ancient Mind-Set

The first step we must take to read the Bible as true, as God's story, is to read it with an ancient mind-set. I don't underestimate the difficulty of doing this. Most of us have been shaped by a Greek mind-set. Like the Greeks, we are given to intellectual analysis. We want to categorize and systematize everything in life. We want to "have a place for everything and have everything in its place." We want order, and we want to understand life and control it. We bring this mind-set to the Bible and insist on controlling how it is to be interpreted. We stand over the Bible and become the judge of its truthfulness.

We must remember the roots of Christianity are Hebrew, not Greek. Jesus was a Jew. So were his disciples. Paul, the most important interpreter of the life and work of Jesus, was a Jew. Yes, the early church quickly spread into Rome, into the Hellenistic culture, later among the slaves, and into the African, Spanish, European, and North American cultures, to name a few. And yes, in every culture the Christian faith takes on aspects of that culture. Sometimes the culture into which Christianity has become contextualized reshapes and even distorts the Christian message. The Bible then gets read through the culture. That's what has happened in America and throughout the Western world. We corrupt the Bible when we turn it into a manifesto for the American way of life, for individualism, for consumerism, for political clout.

If we are going to stand *within* and *under* the Bible as the ancients did, we must turn our backs on the Greek insistence on intellectualizing, categorizing, and controlling the Bible. We must begin to read the Bible holistically, relationally, and passionately.

The fathers did not see life as a split between the sacred and the secular. For them everything is sacred. In the Greek mind-set, which I reject, prayer and a relationship to God constitute the sacred part of life separate from work, fun, marriage, or relationships, which constitute the secular part of life. This approach sets aside moments to "get alone with God." However, the ancient, biblical mind-set sees the whole day and indeed all of life—work, fun, marriage, and relationships—as the realm of the sacred. God is everywhere, at all places, in all times. There is no escaping the presence of God, for God's Spirit is the one who gives life to all of life. This holistic mind-set takes history seriously and sees God as involved in all of history from beginning to end. God calls forth Israel and the church. God is present in the Exodus event and the Christ event and in the formation of a people. God gives Israel direct signs of his presence in the pillar of smoke, in fire, in parted waters, in tablets of stone, in a tabernacle beautifully appointed, in sacrifices, in the Sabbath, in festivals, and in prophets, priests, and kings. In the church God's presence is in the assembled people, in their song, Scripture, water, bread, wine, and oil. God is not an absent, ethereal essence who sits in the sky and demands worship. God is the God who acts, who lives and moves and has his being in the world and among the people. Affirm that all of life, not just part of life, is sacred. Affirm that God is disclosed in every detail of human existence. Then, stand inside the Bible and God's story and let it teach you to look out into the creation where God is signified everywhere yet particularized in Jesus, the ultimate icon of God.

2. Read and Preach the Bible Relationally and Passionately

To stand within the Bible and under it, we must also read the Bible relationally. The Hebrew mind does not describe God intellectually in the abstract as though God is an object to be studied. Instead he is always pictured as the God who enters into a relationship with his creatures. Whether we are standing alongside Adam and Eve, Noah, Abraham and Sarah, Moses and Miriam, David and the kings, or Isaiah and the prophets, God is always visualized in relationship. When God is asked for a name, he responds with the most personal of all names: "I AM WHO I AM" (Exod. 3:14). God's relationship to Israel is always pictured in the language of relationships—father, mother, husband, son, daughter, friend. When Israel goes apostate and wanders away from God, the apostasy and sin of Israel is always described as a broken relationship—a broken marriage, an unfaithful spouse, an erring child. The New Testament images of God and the church continue with the same emphasis on relationship. The church is the "body of Christ," the "bride of Christ," the "community," the "household of faith," the "fellowship in faith." To stand within the Bible, then, read it saying, "I stand in the tradition of the relationship Adam, Abraham, Moses, David, Elizabeth, Mary, and Paul had with God." Reading Scripture from inside the story of God revolutionizes it from a mere factual story (to be proven or demythologized) to a commentary of God working in the world to accomplish his own vision. We then find our place in the vision of God.

Furthermore, to stand within the Bible and to live under it, we must learn, like the Hebrews, to read the Bible passionately—to read the Bible with the heart. The intellect always dissects, makes judgments, analyzes, and sifts, but the heart listens, sees, feels, loves, fears, and believes. References to the heart throughout the Hebrew and early church Scriptures are too numerous to recount. The direction of life is determined in the passions of the heart. After the fall, God saw that "every inclination of [man's] heart is evil from childhood" (Gen. 8:21). Those who turned toward God did so with their heart. Worshipers of God cried, "I will praise you, O LORD, with all my heart; I will tell of all your wonders. I will be glad and rejoice in you; I will sing praise to your name, O Most High" (Ps. 9:1). When Israel turned from God, he proclaimed, "I will give them a heart to know me, that I am the LORD. They will be my people, and I will be their God, for they will return to me with all their heart" (Jer. 24:7). The church and each of us as the "people of God" are to "love the Lord your God with all your heart and with all your soul and with all your strength and with all your mind" (Luke 10:27), for "where your treasure is, there your heart will be also" (Luke 12:34).

3. Read and Preach the Bible as Metaphor

There is another Hebrew characteristic that will help us read the Bible with new eyes. It is to read the Bible out of the language of metaphor, poetry, pictures, story, and paradox. Unfortunately, the Western approach to language is primarily that of the Romans—precise, terse, and factual. This kind of language gets parsed, diagrammed, dissected, and analyzed. But the Hebrew language is more imaginative, ambiguous, and evocative. Language is more than words that make up sentences; it also includes forms and styles of communication. For example, when we read the Bible with our Western mind-set, we tend to reshape the various forms of Hebrew imagination into propositional statements. But the Hebrew way of communicating cannot be reduced to propositions that can be managed and controlled.

The Hebrews speak, for example, through metaphors that draw on the senses. Instead of fixating on concrete language that can always be understood as factual, they use colorful metaphors that communicate in imaginative ways. Marvin Wilson points out:

127

"look" is to "lift up the eyes" (Gen. 22:4); "be angry" is "burn in one's nostrils" (Exod. 4:14); "disclose something to another" or "reveal" is "unstop someone's ears" (Ruth 4:4); have no "compassion" is "hard-heartedness" (1 Sam. 6:6); "stubborn" is "stiff-necked" (2 Chron. 30:8; cf. Acts 7:51); "get ready" or "brace oneself" is "gird up the loins" (Jer. 1:17); and "to be determined to go" is "set one's face to go" (Jer. 42:15, 17; cf. Luke 9:61).[4]

At least one-third of the Bible is poetry.

We sometimes forget that the Bible was not available to the ancients. Today we have so many translations and study Bibles available in our homes that the Bible has become almost commonplace. But in the ancient world, the Bible was to be committed to memory, and poetry lent itself to memory. Hebrew poetry is full of parallelisms, simile, personification of nature, imitation of sounds, as well as rhyme and meter. The Western mind often wants to literalize poetry. For example, the creation accounts of Genesis are liturgical poetry, not history or science. What is literal about this poetry is that *God did it*, and because God created, the creation has meaning. When we insist, as some do, that the creation account be turned into a science of the origins of the world, we lose the heart and soul of the poetic message and turn a liberating and imaginative poem into a dry intellectual fact that must be affirmed scientifically. This deadens truth.

The ancient mind is not a lifeless analytical or systematic mind but a picture mind. The Hebrews describe what "the eye sees, rather than what the mind speculates."[5] They don't speak of God in the abstract ways we do in the Western world. Hebrews never set forth arguments for the existence of God. They don't debate the nature of God or view God as an abstract object to be analyzed. Rather, God is always visualized as the "God who acts." The biblical God is not an essence that "sits in the heavens," but a personality who creates, enters into relationship, feels, responds, and interacts. God enters into relationship and finally enters into our own suffering to deliver us from the misery that evil brings. He renews us to his original intent for creation where we find our place in his world.

Perhaps this is why the ancient way of communication is through storytelling. Hebrew stories center around characters who speak for themselves. The whole history of Israel is a story—stories about the beginning of the world, a story about the fall, stories of how rebellious people unfolded culture, stories of God's interaction with Abraham and the patriarchs, stories of how God rescued the Hebrew people from Pharaoh, stories of how God formed them into a people and gave them the law to live by, the tabernacle and its sacrificial system to worship by, the wilderness to test them, and the Promised Land as their place of dwelling. The entire history of the Hebrew people is the story of how God prepared the world to receive his Son, whose story fulfilled all the images and prophecies of the Hebrew people, so that through their history, the Messiah would come to complete the story of the world. This very same story continues in the life of the church and in our very lives today as we discern what God is doing in our time and place in history. In Hebrew history it was the story of expectation; since Christ, it is now the story of fulfillment and the new expectation of God's completed purpose for all creation and creatures in the new heavens and new earth.

The ancient language is also one of paradox. In paradox we always see two sides of the story. God is the actor in all the stories of Israel, but so is Israel and individuals within Israel. So the narrative always has both a divine side and a human side. God chooses, calls, elects. God lives among the people speaking, chastising, directing. But the people live in the presence of God, who is among them. They respond and relate to God. They sometimes ignore God or outright disobey God and chase after gods of their own making. But God is always there.

Western thought—especially Enlightenment thinking—does not like paradox. Rational language cannot see how opposites are two sides of the same reality. So some want to read the Bible from the divine side emphasizing divine predestination and divine foreknowledge, but others approach the Bible emphasizing the human side of freedom and choice. In the Hebrew mind both are real and valid. While Hebrews are more than willing to affirm what seems to be a contradiction, the mind-set of modernity refuses to embrace ambiguity and the uncertainty generated by the paradox of both the human and divine face appearing as the two sides of everything everywhere.

4. *Read and Preach the Bible So That It Reads Us and Our World*

What I have been describing above is that the Bible reads me. If Jesus Christ is truly the central figure of the Bible and the one who defines the true spiritual life, then Jesus reads me and the entire world. To read the Bible Christologically is to let it read us and the world. It has the power to read us and the world because the text discloses the waywardness of the human heart. We should not read the accounts of human rebellion against God as the study of "some other person" or of "that particular culture." Instead those accounts, while rooted in a particular history, reach across time to say, "You are there; that's a description of your life, of your sin and rebellion, of your journey away from God, of your world's rebellion." For example, how do the stories of Adam and Eve, Cain and Abel, Noah, the Tower of Babel, Abraham and Sarah, Hagar and Ishmael, Lot and his daughters, Isaac and Rebekah, Jacob and Esau, Rachel and Leah read us? What about the Genesis account of widespread wickedness, or the narrative of kings, judges, and prophets? Is it possible to pick up the Bible and say, "I'm going to read about myself and my world"? Is it possible to say, "I identify with this person; my world is like this; I hear what God said to this community and to this person in this circumstance"? Can we hear God's voice speak to us out of biblical circumstances? Can the Bible be read as our own story from Genesis to Revelation? The Bible tells two stories woven into one grand narrative. It is an interactive story of God and humanity. It reveals truth about God, but it also reveals truths about persons, societies, cultures, and civilization. When we read and preach the Bible as a history present, we get inside of it, and it reads us and our world.

The Bible also reads us because Jesus, who is our Redeemer, is also the model for our true living. Because it is Christ who lives in us, we are to live "in Christ," in his incarnation, in his crucifixion, in his resurrection, in his ascension, and in his coming again. To read the Bible from the inside is to open ourselves to the person the Bible is all about and let that person and his saving work live in us. We live in Christ's re-creative work all the time. We also take time to remember his saving deeds and anticipate his ultimate rule over all in our daily, weekly, and Christian year worship.

130

Conclusion

In this chapter I have pointed to a misguided approach to the reading and preaching of Scripture in worship. When Scripture is read and preached, it all too often is interpreted from the outside rather than from inside the narrative itself. Seminary education has not been particularly helpful. Seminaries influenced by modernity spend too much time on historical criticism, defending biblical truth without adequately teaching truth in depth. Pastors and church leaders influenced by subjective experientialism are too quick to choose verses out of the context of God's great drama and turn those verses into inspirational, motivational, or therapeutic talks.

The apostolic and ancient fathers' way of reading and preaching Scripture is a corrective to the problems cited above. The ancient fathers stood inside the story and interpreted the story out of the dynamic activity of the Triune God. They saw Jesus Christ as the central figure of creation, incarnation, and re-creation.

My challenge to today's pastors, leaders, and Bible interpreters is to rediscover the ancient way of reading and preaching Scripture. Put yourself into the ancient mind-set that allows for narrative, mystery, and typology. This old way of thinking moves us away from our dependence on modern modes of thinking and corresponds more with a postmodern mind-set. Learn to read and preach the Bible relationally as in the community of the Triune God and his reflective community—Israel and the church. Read and preach passionately—knowing that the Word is not mere fact but the spring of divine life interpreting our daily life and all of history. Read and preach Scripture as a metaphor. Allow the pictures of Scripture to emerge in such a way that Scripture and life are seen whole. Read and preach so that all of us stand under the Bible and allow it to read our daily life, our habits, our thoughts, and our actions. Where this kind of reading and preaching of Scripture is seriously and effectively done, the people who live in the wasteland of biblical neglect, thirsty and hungry for the Word to interpret and guide their lives in a crumbling world, will find a way to be there and drink deeply from the well of God's narrative.

7

Eucharist

Transformed by the Presence of God at Table

A few years ago my friend Chuck Fromm, the editor of *Worship Leader* magazine, said, "Bob, face it, the Eucharist was the focal point of God's presence in the ancient church, the Reformation made the Word the center of God's presence, and today the presence of God is found in music."

I believe music-centered worship has indeed become a common way of thinking about the presence of God. However, it is an extremely limited understanding of God's presence. God is everywhere by virtue of creation and his sustaining power. God can be discerned in the beauty of a landscape, in the setting of the sun, or in the face of a baby. But God has told us that "where two or three come together in my name, there I am with them" (Matt. 18:20). The church has always believed not only that God is everywhere but also that he is made intensely present to his church at worship. God is there in the gathering of the assembly, in song, in Scripture reading, in prayer, and especially at bread and wine. Jesus told his disciples that there is a way to remember him (the force of *anamnēsis*

133

is "to make me [Christ] present"). He is right there at broken bread and poured-out wine.

But there has been a failure among Christians shaped by Enlightenment rationalism to see any supernatural divine presence at Table worship. Instead, Table worship is almost always conceived as something *I* do.

The Crisis of Table Worship

The central crisis is the desupernaturalization of Table worship. A student expresses this attitude toward the Eucharist in a paper written for one of my classes:

> It seems to me that the sacrament of communion (sacrament being "a ritualistic practice instituted by God") is more of a *reminding* symbol of Christ's redemptive work, purposed for the sake of *memory* as Jesus said, "Do this in *remembrance of me*" (Luke 27:19, emphasis added).... Would you consider explaining and defending your view on the "doctrine of real presence"? ... If it is to serve as the foundational assertion from which you deduce the meaning and value of Eucharist, it would be helpful to me to read some discussion and support of it before I'm asked to build on it.[1]

What this student is looking for is a rational explanation of "Christ enters us and we him" in the taking of bread and wine.

The Problem of Rationalism

How should we approach the crisis of evangelical doubt, the failure to affirm the communication of Christ at Table worship? The primary way to see the crisis at Table worship is to place it in the larger process of the desupernaturalization of the entire Christian story at the hands of Enlightenment rationalism.

First, the Reformer Zwingli wrenched the Eucharist from its supernatural nature by giving it the status of a memorial, which makes it something *we* do. Then during the eighteenth and nineteenth centuries the Bible was humanized by historical and literary criticism and turned into the product of human search for God. The Bible was no longer seen as a revelation from God. More recently, the incarnation of God in Christ has been replaced with a human Jesus, and the supernatural implications of the death and resurrection of Jesus have been reinterpreted as myths having no historical, atoning, or reconciling significance.

Obviously, evangelical Christians are not to be associated with the liberal and mythological interpretation of Christianity. Evangelicals affirm that God has created, revealed, become incarnate, died, rose, ascended, and will return again. Evangelical supernaturalism, however, is often limited to these parts of God's story as *interventions* in creation that need to be proven by the test of an evidential apologetic. By not affirming a complete supernaturalism in which God is always and everywhere present in creation, evangelicals are in danger of the eventual breakdown of all supernaturalism and possible retooling of the faith to not only look like the culture but even embrace a new form of secularized Christianity.

This steady march toward a new antisupernatural faith is already evident in worship and spirituality. A study of contemporary worship songs demonstrates that the current view of worship is not situated in God's supernatural story. Instead, worship is situated within the worshiper and is offered by the worshiper to God, who often remains unnamed in the song lyrics. Furthermore, many popular books and retreats on spirituality focus on the journey of the self. They assume that spirituality lies within the self and that one can find the spiritual self by going deep into the self to release or awaken a latent spiritual condition. This divorce of worship and spirituality from God's story of creation, incarnation, and re-creation has resulted in a new kind of Gnostic worship and spirituality. The denial of a consistent supernaturalism in which God is disclosed not only in Jesus and in Scripture but also at bread and wine is a clash of vision. To say that God is not communicated to us through visible and tangible signs such as gatherings of people, the words of Scripture, and the material reality of water, bread, and wine is a rejection of creation as the handiwork of God. Ultimately, if carried to its conclusion, this view will reject that God was united to human flesh in the incarnation. The mystery of faith embraces the reality of the incarnation and an incarnational presence in the bread and wine.

A Worldview Clash

Do we live in a supernatural world in which the Creator and Redeemer of all things actively discloses the relationship he has initiated and established with us, or do we live in a natural world where God chooses not to reveal himself? Evangelicals, like my student quoted earlier, *do* believe we live in a supernatural world, but they limit God's disclosure to an inspired Bible, the incarnation, death, and resurrection, and the conversion experience. The ancient church and the Reformers embraced a much larger supernaturalism, affirming that God is revealed in all of creation in a general way and intensely revealed in salvation history (Israel and Jesus) and that this disclosure of himself continues in the church through the visible signs of his presence in worship, especially at bread and wine.

In order to address the questions asked by my student, it is necessary to place the Table worship of bread and wine back into the story of God. The entire story is supernatural. It presupposes the paradox that the transcendent God who is above and beyond creation is yet immanent in (within) creation. As we have seen, God's otherness, his quality of being invisible, is made visible in the incarnation.

But then the biblical story never seeks to prove itself. It is a given that "in the beginning God created the heavens and the earth" (Gen. 1:1), and from there through the book of Revelation everything is seen from a supernatural perspective. Whether we read of God creating or the calling of Abraham, the Exodus event, the formation of Israel with its worship and laws, the prophets, the incarnation of God in Jesus, the ministry of Jesus, his death, resurrection, ascension, and present priestly ministry, his return to establish the new heavens and new earth—it is all supernatural. It is not here and there that one sees a supernatural intrusion into history. It is all from beginning to end couched in the commitment that everywhere throughout creation and in all things God is known and made present. The person through whom we see the world and its history in all its ultimate glory is Jesus Christ in whom heaven and earth meet, for in him the divine and the human are united and in him and through his death and resurrection all creation—including our own lives—is transfigured.

136

Far from being a mere memorial or empty symbol, the ancient fathers saw bread and wine as a disclosure of Jesus Christ, through whom we see the reconciliation of God and man, of heaven and earth, and of all things. But Enlightenment rationalism has succeeded in taking the focus off what God does at bread and wine and placing it on what I do at bread and wine. In rationalism, I must make Table worship a source of spiritual nourishment by what I do. I must remember. The more intense my remembrance, the more my spiritual life is nourished. Is it really true that I nourish myself at the Table? Or are we moderns missing something here at the Table—something God may be doing to nourish our spiritual life? The ancient fathers speak to this crisis.

Bread and Wine in the Ancient Church

The early church fathers did not see bread and wine as a mere human reminder of Jesus. Instead they approached bread and wine with a clear sense of the supernatural.

Ignatius

Ignatius, the bishop of Antioch in AD 110, is our first example. Ignatius, who may have known some of the apostles, especially John, was taken by the Roman authorities to the Roman arena to be put to death. En route he wrote seven letters to the leaders of the churches in Asia Minor—Ephesus, Magnesia, Tralles, Rome, Philadelphia, Smyrna—and to Polycarp, who was later martyred.

Of great concern to Ignatius was the presence of the Gnostics in Asia Minor. Gnostics taught that the incarnation was not a physical, tangible, embodied incarnation of God in human flesh but an *apparition*. It only seemed to be an incarnation. Ignatius insisted on a real, enfleshed incarnation of God. He wrote to the Trallians:

> Be deaf to any talk that ignores Jesus Christ, of David's lineage, of Mary, who was really born, ate, and drank; was really persecuted under Pontius Pilate; was really crucified and died, in the sight of heaven and earth and the underworld. He was really raised from the dead, for his Father raised him, just as his Father will raise us,

who believe on him, through Christ Jesus, apart from whom we have no genuine life.[2]

The key to eucharistic thought in the writings of Ignatius is the embodied reality of the incarnation. He addresses the Gnostics out of an incarnational perspective and applies the incarnation to eucharistic thinking. He warns the Smyrneans to stay away from the Gnostics, who teach "wrong notions about the grace of Jesus Christ." This is evident in their bias against the physical and material dimension of the gospel, not only in the incarnation of God in the flesh but also in their neglect of the poor and of the Eucharist.

> They care nothing about love: they have no concern for widows or orphans, for the oppressed, for those in prison or released, for the hungry or the thirsty. They hold aloof from the Eucharist and from services of prayer, because they refuse to admit that the Eucharist is the flesh of our Saviour Jesus Christ, which suffered for our sins and which, in his goodness, the Father raised [from the dead].[3]

Ignatius sees bread and wine from a supernatural perspective. This is evident in other comments about the Eucharist. In his letter to the Trallians he speaks of the "deacons of Jesus Christ's 'mysteries' [bread and wine]" as those who "do not serve mere food and drink, but minister to the church."[4] He encourages the church at Ephesus to "gather together more frequently to celebrate God's Eucharist and to praise him. For when you meet with frequency, Satan's powers are overthrown and his destructiveness is undone by the unanimity of your faith. There is nothing better than peace, by which all strife in heaven and earth is done away."[5] His advice to the Ephesian Christians is to "break one loaf, which is the antidote which wards off death but yields continuous life in union with Jesus Christ."[6] Ignatius also wrote to the Philadelphians, "Be careful, then, to observe a single Eucharist. For there is one flesh of our Lord, Jesus Christ, and one cup of his blood that makes us one, and one altar."[7]

Finally, as he approaches Rome and certain death at the teeth of the lions, Ignatius urges the Romans not to prevent his martyrdom. "For though alive," he says, "it is with a passion for death that I am writing to you. . . . What I want is God's bread, which is the flesh of Christ, who came from David's line, and for drink I want his blood: an immortal feast indeed."[8]

What is clear in the writings of Ignatius is that he, like the apostles, believes that Jesus Christ was God incarnate in our flesh, and that his death and resurrection were real, actual, earthed, and embodied. The crucifixion and resurrection happened in time, space, and history. He then applies the embodied incarnation to the visible symbols of Christ's saving presence in the assembled community and argued if God has become incarnate in human flesh, then a real presence of Christ is manifested in bread and wine. He does not state how God is made present at bread and wine. It is a mystery, like the incarnation itself.

Justin Martyr

Like Ignatius, second-century apologist Justin Martyr was martyred for his faith. Also like Ignatius, he approached the supernatural nature of what happened at bread and wine as an application of the incarnation.

Justin's letter, known as the "First Apology of Justin, the Martyr," was a defense of Christianity against the critics. The letter was presented to Emperor Titus with the hope that by understanding the practices of Christianity the emperor would cease persecuting the church. It had been rumored that Christians sacrificed and ate infants in their worship as an offering to their God. This rumor prompted Justin to describe Christian worship, and especially the worship of God with bread and wine. Here is his description of the meaning of bread and wine:

> For we do not receive these things as common bread or common drink; but as Jesus Christ our Saviour being incarnate by God's word took flesh and blood for our salvation, so also we have been taught that the food consecrated by the word of prayer which comes from him, from which our flesh and blood are nourished by transformation, is the flesh and blood of that incarnate Jesus.[9]

The incarnational nature of Justin's description of Table worship is made more clear by a diagram of its content. Consider the following comparison Justin makes between the occurrence of the incarnation and the prayer of consecration over bread and wine.

Not Common Bread or Drink

Incarnation	Consecration
Jesus Christ our Savior	Food
Incarnate by God's Word	Consecrated by word of prayer
Took flesh and blood	From which our flesh and blood
For our salvation	Nourished by transformation

is
the flesh and blood of that
incarnate Jesus

Justin is presenting the same incarnational view of bread and wine in AD 150 that we met in Ignatius forty years earlier.

Justin makes a parallel between the incarnation and the consecration. Just as the incarnation assures us that Jesus Christ our Savior was incarnate by God's word and took flesh and blood for our salvation, so also we can be certain that "the food consecrated by the word of prayer" is the food from which our flesh and blood is nourished by transformation. It is for this reason that bread and wine are not common bread or drink but "the flesh and blood of that incarnate Jesus."

The statement "is the body and blood of Jesus" should not be interpreted as transubstantiation—a view that was not affirmed until the thirteenth century by the Roman Catholic Church. Rather, it would be more appropriate to describe the ancient view of God's presence at bread and wine this way: an incarnational and supernatural dimension is attributed to bread and wine. When bread and wine are received in faith, we are transformed. Bread and wine nourish our union with Jesus. It transforms us into his image and likeness.

The testimony of the early church fathers is clear: the Christian faith is a supernatural vision of reality. God is known to us through bread and wine, for these elements, together with the prayers that surround their celebration disclose Christ in all of his saving and transforming presence, both as he is prefigured in the Old Testament and as he is anticipated in his future final victory over all that is sin and death in the world.

140

Bread and Wine Disclose Christ and Transform Us in His Image

It is imperative that we identify the divine disclosure that occurs at Table worship and ask how it nourishes us. What is disclosed at God's Table touches us on many levels and nourishes us in many ways.

The Whole Story of God

At bread and wine God discloses his whole story for those who know how to see. Yes, bread and wine are symbols, but they are not empty. The ancient fathers taught that symbols participate in the reality they re-present. We do not make a symbol meaningful by ascribing a meaning to it, as the Enlightenment teaches. Instead meaning inheres within a symbol because a symbol signifies a reality and performs that reality. Bread and wine signify and perform God's story and communicate the benefits of God's story to us. When we open our hearts, our minds, and our wills to see ourselves inside God's story, to think God's thoughts after him, and to embody God's story in love, we become broken bread and poured out wine to others in an incarnate, cruciform, resurrected, and eschatological life.

Therefore, while the Bible discloses the story of the world in words, the same story is enacted at bread and wine. Rationalism cannot embrace this, for it only sees bread as food that is eaten and wine as drink that is imbibed. But when we come to the Table with the eyes of faith, we experience the burning conviction that we live in a supernatural world. We no longer see bread and wine as mere elements of the earth but as symbols that reveal the story of the universe. At bread and wine we see creation, fall, incarnation, death, resurrection, ascension, church, the kingdom, and the promise of the new heavens and new earth and our own transfiguration accomplished through God's union with us established through Jesus by the Spirit.

The Goodness of Creation

Bread and wine, which are the very stuff of God's creation, also signify to us the goodness of God's creative act. What God has made is not intrinsically evil but is capable of being united to God. Therefore, at bread and wine God discloses the union of heaven and earth,

141

the divine and the human, the invisible and the visible, the uncreated and the created. The truth that God is incomprehensible in his very essence is in no way compromised by the conviction that the very presence of God is communicated through the visible, concrete reality of creation (Rom. 1:20). Jewish spirituality is deeply rooted in the consciousness of God's presence experienced in creation without being pantheistic. Christian spirituality stands in the Jewish tradition of affirming God's presence in creation and goes one step further to declare that the God of transcendence is united to creature and creation in the incarnation. As Teilhard de Chardin says, "By virtue of the Creation and, still more, of the Incarnation, *nothing here below is profane* for those who know how to see."[10] There is no rational proof, however, that the presence of God is communicated through bread and wine. Nor would the ancient church embrace explanations of God's presence at bread and wine such as the Roman Catholic doctrine of transubstantiation, the Lutheran doctrine of consubstantiation, or the Calvinistic view that the Eucharist is a sign, witness, or testimony to God's presence. Instead, for one who affirms an ancient-future worship, the presence of Christ at bread and wine is a mystery situated in the larger mystery of the entire story of God's relationship to the world. As God is revealed in all of creation, in sacred Scripture, in Jesus and in the church, so God is revealed at bread and wine. But what do we see?

The Union of God and Humanity

Bread and wine reveal that creatures and creation find their completion and fulfillment in union with the divine. Until we are united with the divine, we go it alone with the focus on self. We seek meaning in the self but find that we are laced with dysfunction in the interior person and in all the complexities of society. Bread and wine reveal there is only one person, Jesus, in whom the divine and human meet and through whom our own union with the divine is accomplished. Here at bread and wine God reveals how our union with him is accomplished. For Jesus, who shares in our humanity yet is united to God, took bread and wine and said, "This is my body. . . . This is my blood . . . poured out for many for the forgiveness of sins" (Matt. 26:26, 28). Look at bread and wine

142

not as common bread and drink but as the image of the union of the human and the divine, "For the sake of our salvation" (Nicene Creed), now disclosed in the common elements of bread and wine that sustain our life in this world and the next.

The Sacrifice of Christ

In my experience, most Christians seem to be very clear on how bread and wine point to the sacrificial death of Jesus. Drawing from the Hebrews' sacrificial system, these Christians point to the once and for all sacrifice of Christ on the cross as a fulfillment of all the Old Testament types. I affirm, with the liturgies of the early church, that his sacrifice was voluntary. I do not, like some feminists, see the suffering of Christ on the cross as an "abuse" by his father, nor do I see his suffering as coerced or determined. His self-sacrifice came from his genuine struggle with death in the Garden of Gethsemane. But unlike the choice made by Adam in a garden to go his own way, Jesus chose "not my will, but yours be done" (Luke 22:42). He willingly chose the way of the cross as an act of love. For God so loved the world that he was willing to give himself as a sacrifice. The sacrifice of himself for the reconciliation of the world was already taking place in the womb of the Virgin Mary. When the divine united with the human within the womb, all creatures and creation are present in the humanity of Jesus. The sacrifice had begun. His sacrifice continued on earth where he suffered rejection by his own creation in spite of the continual manifestation of his love in his teachings, his miracles, and his identification with the poor, the oppressed, and the outcasts of society. Then, in his final act of sacrifice, he gave his own life, the shedding of his own blood, the death of his own body for the sake of the world. Ancient prayers refer to the cross as "the life-giving cross" because his poured-out life flows into us and gives us life. His blood, which is the life of the flesh, grants us a new life, a new beginning, and it makes us new creatures refashioned after his image.

We are nourished by the image of Jesus's sacrifice, for it manifests to us our union with him in his sufferings. His life of sacrifice is to become our life of self-giving, for we abide in him and he in us (John 15:4). The one true fulfilled and meaningful life is not the life of acquisition, power, fame, sexual freedom, consumerism, or

143

materialism but the cruciform life. The spiritual life is lived out of the crucifixion. It is a willing, voluntary choosing to give oneself to others, to endure suffering for the needs of others, even, if necessary, to the point of death. Table worship nourishes this commitment because it discloses the meaning of life as the act of giving up self in order to do the will of God for others.

A Victory over the Powers of Evil

At bread and wine Christ is manifested as the Victor over sin and death, the Conqueror over the devil and all that is rebellious against God. At bread and wine we see Jesus as Lord of heaven and earth, ruling his creation in love. This disclosure nourishes our anticipation in a world that is not yet visibly under the rule of Christ. For through bread and wine we see the hope of a world transfigured, renewed, and restored.

The earliest Christian eucharistic prayer triumphantly proclaims, "He was betrayed to voluntary suffering that he might destroy death, and break the bonds of the devil, and tread down hell, and shine upon the righteous, and fix a term [i.e., the powers of evil are bound and limited and can only function within the boundary set by God], and manifest the resurrection."[11] Bread and wine manifest the resurrection, the new beginning that God has established for creatures and creation. It is to be seen in the church, the body of Christ, the community called to be the new humanity. This new community of God's people on earth witness to the overthrow of evil (Eph. 3:10) in their worship and in their lives (1 Peter 2:9–12). They live into the future of the new heavens and new earth (2 Peter 3:8–18) in full conviction that the bread and wine, which foreshadow the coming of Christ (Matt. 26: 29; 1 Cor. 11:26), evoke the prayer, "Your kingdom come, your will be done on earth as it is in heaven" (Matt. 6:10).

The Redemption of the Whole World

Not only does the celebration of bread and wine manifest the work of God to redeem creatures and creation, it also presents the whole world to God through Jesus Christ. When the minister lifts the bread and wine heavenward and declares "The body of Christ given for you, . . . The blood of Christ poured out for you," the whole earth and all creatures are presented to God. God is asked to remember the world and the sacrifice he himself made, to remember that he "so loved the world that he gave his one and only Son, that whoever believes in him shall not perish but have eternal life" (John 3:16).

Bread and wine reveal God's intent for the whole world. The offering and sacrifice of Christ is meant to manifest the church as God's new creation. Bread and wine manifest to the world its own ultimate destiny. Bread and wine are a glorious display of the union of heaven and earth, the visible and the invisible, the overcoming of the powers, and the transfigured glory of the new heavens and new earth.

God Remembers

The remembrance that happens at the Table is not only that our remembering makes Christ present but also that God himself is reminded what he has done to redeem and restore the union of himself to creatures and creation. We rely on the attentiveness of God to his own memory as the primary memorial of bread and wine and then to our own participation in his memory as the nourishing and sustaining feature of "Do this in remembrance of me" (1 Cor. 11:24–25). Alexander Schmemann expresses this thought clearly:

> Here we should recall that in the biblical, Old Testamental teaching on God, the term memory refers to the attentiveness of God to his creation, the power of divine providential love, through which God "holds" the world and *gives it life*, so that life itself can be termed abiding in the memory of God, and death and falling out of this memory. In other words, memory, like everything else in God, is *real*, it *is* that life that he grants, that God "*remembers*"; it *is* the eternal overcoming of the "nothing" out of which God called us into his wonderful light.[12]

Memory is not a mere recall, like we would remember a friend or a significant event in our life, but a remembrance that unfolds the whole meaning of life and of the cosmos. This memory is re-presented and disclosed at bread and wine to form us and so thoroughly shape our perception of life and the world that it empowers

145

our living and inescapably and profoundly effects our living in union with Jesus Christ.

Application

What nourishes and transforms us at bread and wine is the disclosure of the whole story of God—creation, incarnation, re-creation—which takes up residence inside of us as we take and eat, take and drink. For in this symbol a reality is present—the divine action of God redeeming his world through Jesus Christ; the calling for us to see that our union with God, and indeed the union of all heaven and earth, is accomplished by God alone in Jesus Christ. In eating and drinking we experience a foretaste of the supper of the Lamb in the kingdom of Christ's rule over heaven and earth (Revelation 19). We become what we eat—living witnesses to Christ who lives in us.

How does Christ enter into us and we into him? I suggest we reflect on the spiritual disciplines of contemplation and participation as they relate to the receiving of bread and wine.

In order to contemplate Christ at bread and wine, many will have to go through a paradigm shift because we are so deeply formed by Enlightenment rationalism that we only see common bread and wine. We live with such a truncated and desupernaturalized faith that we want a *reason* to believe that Jesus is disclosed at bread and wine. In this demand we do what I have been decrying from the start of this book. We bring our Enlightenment worldview to God's story and demand that God's story be accountable to reason and science. We must denounce the priority we give to a false worldview and step into the story of God and see bread and wine from *within* the story. The story says, "You do not live in a natural world explained by reason and science." The story says, "You live in a supernatural world of wonder and mystery. Stand in this world and receive the mystery of bread and wine. It discloses the goodness of creation and the union of the human and divine. Bread and wine embody the images of heaven and earth united and the future anticipated restoration of the whole world under Jesus. Be free from the constraints of reason and science and meet the true meaning of life in the mystery of these elements."

146

How do bread and wine draw us into a participation in the life of God in the world? Bread and wine disclose the union we have with Jesus, which is not a mere standing but a true and real participation lived out in this life as we become the story of God in this world individually in all our ways and corporately as the people of God. First, we ingest bread and wine. Then, in contemplation we look on with steadfast delight in all that bread and wine disclose. And then in participation, we reach out and see the whole world in the hands of God. We lift the Alpha and Omega to our mouth. We take God's whole story into our stomach, let it run through our bloodstream, let it then energize our entire living—our relationships, our work, our pleasure; all of life is now to be lived as Jesus lived his life. As he took into himself the suffering of all humanity, so we are to take into ourselves the suffering of the world and do something about it. As he rose above all that is evil in the world through his resurrection, so we too are to rise to the new life by the Spirit of God. All our death to sin and rising to life finds its true and ultimate meaning in him who lives in us, living in our sufferings, living in our struggles with evil, living in our resurrections to new life.

So the celebration of bread and wine is no abstract object out there, no *thing* to be observed as an object of interest, no mere ritual to be taken in a perfunctory or mechanical way. No. We move from a delightful contemplation of all that bread and wine disclose to a participation in God's story by continually affirming in bread and wine that Jesus is given anew and poured out again to the world through our individual lives and through the community of the people of God, the church, who manifest God's purposes for the world in the worship of our lips and lives.

Summary

In this chapter I have argued that the current and long-standing crisis of Table worship is caused by the influence of the Enlightenment. The mystery of God's presence has been lost and replaced with an empty symbolism. Many Christians and even pastors and leaders of the church have acted indifferently to God's presence at Table, transferring it to music or dropping it completely. Remember, for example, the pastor who, after hearing a lecture I gave on God's presence at Table worship, came to me and said, "I love what you had to say. We do communion on New Year's Eve, but I don't think my people would tolerate it more often than that. Could you suggest an alternative that would have the same effect?" This response is tantamount to saying, "I preach from the Bible once a year, but I don't think my people would tolerate it more often. Can you suggest an alternative?" Jesus said there is a way to remember me—it is bread and wine. Why don't we follow the clear teaching of Jesus?

I have suggested that we go back to the earliest common tradition of the ancient fathers. The closest term that fits the ancient fathers' understanding of God's presence at bread and wine is *real presence*. Real presence is a very different view than others developed in history, which are all attempts to explain what cannot be explained. For example, the Roman Catholic doctrine of transubstantiation explains how the divine overshadows the human so that the bread and wine actually becomes the real body and blood of Jesus. The Lutheran doctrine of consubstantiation explains the presence of Christ "in, with, and around" the bread and wine (much like a poker in the fire where the poker becomes red hot with the flame but is not actually the fire). Calvin suggested we see bread and wine as "signs, testimony, and witness" to the activity of God in Jesus to save the world. Zwingli, another Reformer, popularized the notion that the celebration of bread and wine is a "memorial," which desupernaturalized the bread and wine by placing all the action in the faith of the receiver rather than any divine action from above. Bread and wine became the *human attempt* to see God's work in Jesus Christ. The exclusive emphasis on human responsibility is not consistent with the incarnation, where we confess the *union* of 100 percent human and 100 percent divine. From God's perspective bread and wine are a foretaste of the kingdom to come when God's garden is restored and all heaven and earth will be under God's shalom.

Real presence makes no attempt to explain what happens at bread and wine. It affirms the mystery of God's presence at bread and wine even as it affirms the mystery of the union of human and divine in incarnation. We are called, not to understanding, but to the fixed gaze of contemplation and to an active participation in the life of Christ. Herein lies the experience of mystery at bread and wine.

8

Prayer

*Transformed by Recovering the Style
of Ancient Worship*

Do you believe public prayer of the church has the power
to shape who we are and how we behave? By the term
public prayer I do not mean the incidental prayers done here and
there within worship. Rather, *public prayer* refers to the total worship experience, from its beginning to its end. The kind of worship
I refer to is a prayer in the world for the world.

The gathering with its procession, songs of praise, prayers, and
confessions is an act of prayer. The Word with its readings, Psalms,
preaching, prayers of intercession, passing of the peace, and offering is all prayer. The Table worship with its setting, the "holy,
holy, holy," the alleluias, breaking of the bread, offering of the cup,
rites of healing, and songs of death, resurrection, communion, and
thanksgiving is all an act of prayer. The dismissal that sends people
forth to love and serve the Lord is an act of prayer.

These acts of prayer, however, are not a mere collection of prayers
but a praying of God's story of the world and an offering of God's
story of the world to God as an act of thanksgiving. The whole act

149

of worship says, "God, we are here to remember your story and to pray that the whole world, the entire cosmos, will be gathered in your Son and brought to the fulfillment of your purposes in him!" This kind of a prayer is a public way to remember God's saving deeds in the past and to anticipate God's rule over all creation in the future.

The Crisis of Public Prayer

The first crisis of public prayer is its neglect. By *neglect* I do not mean to suggest that congregational worship has no prayer within it. Indeed, most if not all churches will do prayers. They may begin and end with prayer. A prayer may be said before a sermon or at its ending; intercessory prayers may be made for the sick, for shut-ins, for the needs of the congregation, local city, country, and even the world (however, many contemporary churches do not have a place for intercessory prayer). What I speak of here as the neglect of prayer is the failure to conduct all of worship as the prayer of the church for the life of the world.

This failure to grasp all of worship as a cosmic prayer has several underlying causes. The first and, I believe, most fundamental reason why worship is not seen as prayer is the failure to grasp that corporate prayer arises from the story of God. We think of corporate prayers as arising within ourselves. Yet the story of God, as I have presented it throughout this book, is the story of the world and of human existence. Worship prays this story. But this thought and the application of this thought for the content and structure of worship is neglected simply because it is unheard of by many.

A second reason why worship is not seen as the prayer of God's people for the world is because worship has been turned into a program. Worship, influenced by the broadcast communication theories of the media revolution, has become an entertaining presentation. The commitment to worship "programming" has been intensified by the contemporary Christian music industry. Because people are drawn by entertainment, showmanship, and celebrity, many local churches have turned to a presentational worship to attract the masses.

150

Consequently, the nature of worship has shifted from corporate prayer to platform presentational performance. Worship, instead of being a rehearsal of God's saving actions in the world and for the world, is exchanged for making people feel comfortable, happy, and affirmed. Worship, no longer the public prayer of God's people, becomes a private and individual experience. Beneath the privatization of worship is the ever-present individualism of our culture. This focus on the self results in prayers that are concerned with my life, my needs, my desires—prayers that seem indifferent to the needs of the poor and the problem of violence and war that devours nations and societies and ignore the works of God in Christ to bring to an end all evil, death, and sin. So where do we go from here? What can we learn from the ancient church?

Public Prayer in the Ancient Church

Worship as public prayer may be described as follows: "Public prayer lifts up all creation to the Father through Jesus Christ by the Spirit in praise and thanksgiving for the work of the Son, who has reconciled creatures and creation to God." Because this is what the public prayer of the church does, *the story of God is the substance of the inner content that shapes the outer form of public prayer. Worship prays God's story.*

This relationship between the story of God and worship is evident in the worship of Israel. Hebrew public worship is rooted in creation, the Exodus event, the unfolding story of God's relationship with Israel and the hope of the Promised Land, the sacrifices of the tabernacle and the temple, the Passover, and the other yearly cycle events. The Sabbath and all domestic liturgies are shaped in their internal content by God's story in Israel. So it is with Christian prayer.

God's story shapes all parts of public worship. The entire inner structure—the gathering, the Word, the Eucharist, and the dismissal—is shaped by the story of God. In this worship-prayer nothing is incidental, nothing peripheral, nothing ancillary to the story of God. Be it the opening prayer, the Psalms and canticles, the prayer before preaching, preaching itself, the intercessory prayers,

151

the passing of the peace, the eucharistic prayer, the benediction, and all hymns and choruses—all these components of worship fit together as the whole public prayer of the church. This prayer in total lifts the world and all its inhabitants before God in thankful praise for the work of Jesus Christ, through whom the redemption of the world is accomplished. It prays for the completion of God's work for the salvation of the whole world.

This public prayer of the church for the world is always offered to God through Jesus Christ by the Spirit. For it is Jesus Christ who, by the Spirit, unites heaven and earth, God and humanity, the eternal and the temporal, not only by the incarnation, death, and resurrection, but also by being the eternal mediator between God and his world (Heb. 9:24) and the one who finalizes God's story in his return.

This truth, the story of creatures and creation restored through Jesus Christ by the Spirit, which is the substance of eternal worship and prayer, is equally the content and form of earthly prayer and worship. In the next few pages I will demonstrate how the story of God is the content of worship that shapes its outer, public form. Because the full development of the content of worship as God's story shaping its outward form is quite complex, I will limit my comments to illustrate the relationship with a few examples taken from the St. John Chrysostom liturgy. The origins of this liturgy lie in the fourth century.

Worship as Prayer

If the prayer of the church arises from the story of God, then prayer is simultaneously for the world as a whole and for each individual within the world. Alexander Schmemann, a twentieth-century Orthodox liturgist, presents it this way:

> The Great Litany bestows on us, reveals the prayer of the Church, or, still better, *the Church as prayer*, as precisely the "common task," in its full cosmic and universal extent. In the church assembly man is called above all to give up, to "lay aside" his "cares" for everything that is only *his own*, personal, private, and as it were to "dissolve" himself and what is his own in the prayer of the Church. The Great

Litany discloses the Christian "hierarchy of values"; and only to the extent that each participant accepts it as his own can he fulfill his "membership," overcoming that egoism that very often taints and perverts the Church and religious life itself. The personal and the concrete, however, are not excluded from the Church's prayer. And here is the essence of the concluding, Augmented Litany: in it the Church focuses her prayer on the "private," personal needs of men. If in the first case, in the Great Litany, everything private "dies" as it were in the *whole*, then here all the power of the Church's prayer, all her love, is concentrated on *this person*, on his *needs*. But it is only because we could first identify ourselves with the *general*, in the love of Christ, because we could liberate ourselves from our egocentrism, that we can now, through the love of Christ, abiding in the Church, turn to "every Christian soul that is afflicted and weary in well-doing, in need of God's mercy and help." (This petition is found in the vesperal rite.)[1]

Knowing there is a place for individual prayers once the world has been laid in the lap of God, we may turn to how the church prays for the whole life of the world. How is worship the prayer of the church for the redemption of the whole world, the cosmic order of all things, and equally the prayer for each individual within the world? I will quote extensively but not completely from various parts of a contemporary version of the ancient Byzantine liturgy and make a brief commentary on each prayer.[2] However, the prayers, which are long, speak for themselves. Therefore I suggest that instead of reading the prayers, you *pray the prayer and enter into the purpose of each prayer for both the world and for yourself.*

The Rite of Preparation

The ancient service began with a rite of preparation, or a brief service that readied the community for worship. (Not all the people came. Normally these prayers were prayed by the clergy and a group of the laity—the faithful.) The service primarily consisted of three antiphons, a response, and usually a Psalm. Here are the antiphons that constitute the preparation for worship and the response following the third antiphon. As you pray these prayers note: (1) the emphasis on the Triune God, (2) the rule of God over the whole

153

world, and (3) the concern for each individual in the world. You might want to chant these prayers. Chanting slows you down and provides you with the opportunity to spiritually savor every word and phrase.

The First Antiphon
Deacon: Let us pray to the Lord.
People: Lord, have mercy.
Priest: O Lord our God, Whose power is unimaginable and Whose glory is inconceivable, Whose mercy is immeasurable and Whose love for mankind is beyond all words, in Your compassion, O Lord, look down on us and on this holy house, and grant us and those who are praying with us the riches of Your mercy and compassion. For to You are due all glory, honor and worship, to the Father and to the Son and to the Holy Spirit, now and ever and unto ages of ages.
People: Amen.

The Second Antiphon
Deacon: Let us pray to the Lord.
People: Lord, have mercy.
Priest: O Lord our God, save Your people and bless Your inheritance. Guard the fullness of Your Church, sanctify those who love the beauty of Your House, glorify them by Your divine power and do not forsake us who hope in You. For Yours is the dominion and the Kingdom and the power and the glory of the Father and of the Son and of the Holy Spirit, now and ever and unto ages of ages.
People: Amen.

The Third Antiphon
Deacon: Let us pray to the Lord.
People: Lord, have mercy.
Priest: O Lord, Who have given us the grace to pray together in peace and in harmony, and Who promise to grant the requests of two or three who agree in Your Name,

fulfill even now the petitions of Your servants as is best for us, giving us in this age the knowledge of Your truth, and in the age to come, eternal life. For You are good, O our God, and You love mankind, and we send up glory to You, to the Father and to the Son and to the Holy Spirit, now and ever and unto ages of ages.

People: **Amen.**

At the end of the third antiphon the people sing Psalm 93 with the refrain below:

O Only-begotten Son and Word of God, who is immortal, yet did deign for our salvation to be incarnate of the holy Theotokos and ever-virgin Mary, and without change was made man; and was crucified also, O Christ our God, and by your death did Death subdue; who are one of the Holy Trinity, glorified together with the Father and the Holy Spirit: save us.

Note that the content of the refrain is the heart of God's story—the union of God with man to destroy the power of death.

The Liturgy of the Word

The preparatory rite leads into the service of the Word, which is begun with prayers that cover the needs of the world, the church, the nation, the city, weather, and those who travel, and it ends with an emphasis on individuals and a petition that they commit all of life to God. Pray these prayers with the realization that the Scriptures are not yet read and the sermon is not yet preached because the church must first pray for all the world and each person in it. In these words the church is doing its mission to the world by praying for the world's welfare and for its ultimate salvation. The church prays not only for itself and for its people but for the whole world and all the people of the world. The work of Christ to restore union with God extends to the whole world and to all people. Consequently, worship as prayer asks God to be merciful, through Jesus and by the Spirit, to the whole world, the world that God loves and calls back into union with himself.

Deacon: In peace, let us pray to the Lord.
People: Lord, have mercy.
Deacon: For the peace from above and for the salvation of our souls, let us pray to the Lord.
People: Lord, have mercy.
Deacon: For the peace of the whole world, for the stability of the holy churches of God, and for the union of all, let us pray to the Lord.
People: Lord, have mercy.
Deacon: For this holy house and for all who enter with faith, reverence, and the fear of God, let us pray to the Lord.
People: Lord, have mercy.
Deacon: For our Bishop (*N.*), for the honorable priests and deacons in Christ, and for all the clergy and the people, let us pray to the Lord.
People: Lord, have mercy.
Deacon: For this country and for every authority and power within it, let us pray to the Lord.
People: Lord, have mercy.
Deacon: For this city, for every city and country and for the faithful living in them, let us pray to the Lord.
People: Lord, have mercy.
Deacon: For seasonable weather, for an abundance of fruits of the earth, and for peaceful times, let us pray to the Lord.
People: Lord, have mercy.
Deacon: For those who travel by land, air, and sea, the sick and suffering, those under persecution and for their deliverance, let us pray to the Lord.
People: Lord, have mercy.
Deacon: For our deliverance from all affliction, anger, danger, and need, let us pray to the Lord.
People: Lord, have mercy.
Deacon: Help us, save us, have mercy on us and keep us, O God, by Your grace.
People: Lord, have mercy.
Deacon: Remembering our most holy, most pure, most blessed and glorious Lady, the Mother of God, and

Ever-virgin Mary, with all the saints, let us commit
ourselves and each other and all our life unto Christ
our God.

People: **To You, O Lord.**

After the prayers, the service of the Word continues with the
Scripture readings and the sermon. There are more prayers ending
with the prayers for the catechumens. In the ancient church, the
new converts who were going through a time of spiritual training
were dismissed after the sermon to go to another space to engage in
reflection on the Scriptures and sermon. In the meantime, baptized
Christians remained in their places for the Eucharist known as the
"liturgy of the faithful."

The Liturgy of the Faithful (Prayers of the Eucharist)

The prayer that comprises the liturgy of the faithful is far too
lengthy to include in this chapter. It begins with the hymn of the
cherubim, which brings the people from earth into the heavens to
join with the heavenly host in the eternal singing of "the thrice-holy
hymn." The celebrant calls on the faithful to join with the heavenly
host to sing:

> Holy! Holy! Holy! Lord of Hosts! Heaven and earth are filled
> with Your glory. Hosanna in the highest! Blessed is He Who
> comes in the Name of the Lord! Hosanna in the highest!

The prayer then continues to pray God's story, thanking God for
creation, for creating humanity in his image, for becoming involved
in history to restore creation and humanity through Jesus Christ,
who by his death and resurrection has accomplished salvation "for
the life of the world." What I have included below is only a small part
of the total prayer, but it presents the history of God's restoration
of creation with great clarity. It is a prayer that discloses Jesus and
the Spirit as the two hands of God that redeem the world.

> *Celebrant:* (*in a low voice*) With these blessed powers, O
> master and lover of mankind, we sinners also cry
> aloud and say: You are Holy, truly most Holy, and

157

there is no limit to the majesty of Your holiness.
You are just in all Your works, for in righteousness
and true judgment, You have ordered all things for
us. When You had created man by taking dust from
the earth and honored him with Your own image,
O God, You placed him in the paradise of delight,
promising him eternal life and the enjoyment of
everlasting good things in the observance of your
commandments. But when man disobeyed You,
the true God Who created him, and was led astray
by the deceit of the serpent, and died in his own
transgressions, You banished him, in Your righteous
judgment, from paradise into this world. You caused
him to return to the earth from which he was taken,
yet provided for him the salvation of regeneration
in Your Christ Himself. For You did not turn away
forever from the creature You made, O Good One,
and You did not forget the work of Your hands.
Through the tender compassion of Your mercy,
You visited us in manifold ways: You sent us the
prophets; You worked mighty wonders through
Your saints who were pleasing to You in every
generation. You have spoken to us through the
mouths of Your servants the prophets, foretelling to
us the salvation to come. You gave us the law to help
us; You appointed angels to guard us. And when the
fullness of time came, You spoke to us through Your
Son Himself, by Whom You also made the ages. He
is the Radiance of Your glory and the Image of Your
Person. He upholds all things by the word of His
Power. He did not think it robbery to be equal to
You, God and Father. He was God before the ages,
yet He appeared on earth and lived among men. He
took flesh from a holy Virgin; He emptied Himself,
taking the form of a slave. He conformed Himself
to the body of our lowliness in order to conform us
to the image of His glory. For as by man sin entered
into the world, and by sin, death, it pleased Your

Only begotten Son, Who is in Your bosom, God and Father, Who was born of a woman, the holy Mother of God and Ever-virgin Mary, Who was born under the law, to condemn sin in His flesh, so that we who died in Adam might be brought to life in Him Your Christ. He lived as a citizen in this world, and gave us commandments of salvation. He released us from the waywardness of idols and brought us into the knowledge of You, the true God and Father. He won us for Himself as His own chosen people, a royal priesthood, a holy nation. After purifying us with water and sanctifying us with the Holy Spirit, He gave Himself over in exchange to death, in which we were held captive, sold by sin. After descending into hell through the cross, that He might fill all things with Himself, He loosed the bonds of death; He rose on the third day and opened to all flesh the path of resurrection from the dead, since it was not possible for the Author of Life to be dominated by corruption. So He became the firstfruits of those who sleep, the firstborn from among the dead, that He might truly be the first of all things. He ascended into heaven and sits at the right hand of Your majesty on high, and He will come to render to everyone according to his works. And as a memorial of His saving passion, He has left us these things, which we have presented to You according to His command. For when He was about to go forth to His voluntary, blameless, and life-giving death, on the night in which He gave Himself for the life of the world, He took bread into His holy and spotless hands, and when He had presented it to You, His God and Father, He gave thanks, blessed, sanctified, broke it, and

(*aloud*) gave it to His holy disciples and apostles, saying: "Take, eat, this is My body which is broken for you, for the remission of sins."

People: **Amen.**

159

Celebrant: (*in a low voice*) Likewise He took the cup of the fruit
 of the vine and mingled it, gave thanks, blessed and
 sanctified it, and gave it to His holy disciples and
 apostles, saying:

(*aloud*) "Drink of this, all of you! This is My blood of the
 new covenant, shed for you and for many, for the
 remission of sins."

People: **Amen.**

Celebrant: (*in a low voice*) "Do this as a memorial of Me, for as
 often as you eat this Bread and drink this Cup, you
 announce My death and confess My resurrection."
 Therefore, O Master, mindful of His saving passion
 and life-giving cross, His burial for three days and
 resurrection from the dead, His ascension into heaven
 and sitting at Your right hand, O God and Father, and
 His glorious and awesome second coming,

(*aloud*) we offer You Your own, from what is Your own, for
 everyone and for everything.

The liturgy of the faithful continues with the *Epiklesis* (prayer for
the coming of the Holy Spirit), a prayer for the dead (*diptychs*), the
Lord's Prayer, and the prayers at the elevation of bread and wine.
At the receiving of bread and wine the following prayer, which
expresses the spirituality of receiving Jesus and being established
in the new life, is prayed by the person receiving:

Celebrant: O God, save Your people and bless Your
 inheritance.

People: **Amen. Let our mouths be filled with your praise,
 O Lord, that we may sing of your glory: for you
 have permitted us to partake of your holy, divine,
 immortal, and life-giving Mysteries. Establish
 us in your Sanctification, that all the day long we
 may meditate upon your righteousness. Alleluia,
 alleluia, alleluia.**

After receiving the Eucharist, the deacon leads the *Ektenia* (one
more) prayer of thanksgiving. This prayer signals the beginning

160

of the end of the service. It includes the words, "Let us commend ourselves and each other and all our life unto Christ our God." The clergy then recess from the church and end the service with the prayer below, which once again proclaims that God's people have met to bless God, who blesses the world, his church, and every individual:

Deacon: Let us pray to the Lord.
People: **Lord, have mercy.**
Celebrant: O Lord, Who bless those Who bless You, and sanctify those who put their trust in You: save Your people and bless Your inheritance. Protect the whole body of Your Church, and sanctify those who love the beauty of Your house. Glorify them by Your divine power and do not forsake us who hope in You. Give peace to Your world, to Your churches, to the priests, to our civil authorities and to all Your people. For every good gift and every perfect gift is from above, coming down from You, the Father of Lights; and to You we send up glory, thanksgiving, and worship, to the Father and to the Son and to the Holy Spirit, now and ever and unto ages of ages.
People: **Amen.**

This review of the ancient prayers of worship strongly reveals that worship not only contains prayer but *is the prayer of the church for the life of the world and for the welfare and salvation of all its inhabitants.* God's story, revealing the two hands of God through which the world is redeemed by Jesus and the Spirit, is the content and prayer of ancient worship.

Application

I have drawn from the early church to show that the public worship of the church is a prayer of praise and thanksgiving directed, not to the people, but to God. This approach is a paradigm shift from the current presentational notion of worship. Today worship

161

is frequently seen as a presentation made to the people to get them to believe in the first place, to enrich and edify their faith, and to bring healing into their lives. But the ancient church did not design (a contemporary word) worship to reach people, to educate people, or to heal people. Yet in their worship, which was a prayer of praise and thanksgiving offered to God, people were indeed led into contemplation of God's mighty acts of salvation and stimulated to live a life of participation in the life of God in the life of the world. The point is, of course, that how we pray shapes who we are.

One of the strongest proponents of God's story as the shaping content of the spiritual life is the fourth-century Cappadocian father, Gregory of Nyssa (AD 331–394). Gregory embraces the ancient creation, incarnation, and re-creation story. Christ, he argues, is the "source of our growth in the knowledge of God." For he has "united us to himself and restored to us the divine friendship we had at the beginning of time." Therefore, it is his "personal humanity" that "redirects the dynamism of human nature." He follows Athanasius and the other framers of the Nicene Creed in embracing the implication of the incarnation for the spiritual life. "We can be lifted up toward the Most High," he writes, "only if the Lord who lifts up the humble has stooped down to what is below."[3] In the remembrance and anticipation of worship we are moved to contemplate God's mighty deeds of salvation. By contemplating his person and work, we find our own true nature lifted up into a deeper and deeper consciousness of our restored self. Gregory writes:

> If a man's heart has been purified from every creaturely and unruly affection, he will see the Image of the Divine Nature in his own beauty. I think that in this short saying the Word expresses some such counsel as this: There is in you, human beings, a desire to contemplate the true good; but when you hear that the Divine Majesty is exalted above the heavens, that Its glory is inexpressible, Its beauty ineffable, and Its Nature inaccessible, do not despair of ever beholding what you desire. It is indeed within your reach; you have within yourselves the standard by which you apprehend the Divine. For He Who made you did at the same time endow your nature with this wonderful quality. For God imprinted on it the likeness of the glories of His own Nature, as if molding the form of a carving into wax. But the evil that has been poured all around the nature bearing

the Divine Image has rendered useless to you this wonderful thing that lies hidden under vile coverings. If, therefore, you wash off by a good life the filth that has been stuck on your heart like plaster, the Divine beauty will again shine forth in you.

For the Godhead is purity, freedom from passion, and separation from all evil. If therefore these things be in you, God is indeed in you. Hence, if your thought is without any alloy of evil, free from passion, and alien from stain, you are blessed because you are clear of sight. You are able to perceive what is invisible to those who are not purified, because you have been cleansed; the darkness caused by material entanglement has been removed from the eyes of your soul, and so you see the blessed vision radiant in the pure heaven of your heart.[4]

Gregory of Nyssa is describing how contemplation leads to participation in God—seeing and living out our worship. He is not suggesting that any pagan person can recover by self-effort the image of the divine nature. Rather it is God who in Jesus Christ restores and renews human nature so that we may see the blessed vision radiant in the pure heaven of our own heart. How can a contemplation that leads to participation in the life of Christ be attained?

First, we must remember that *worship is a prayer that is focused on historical events.* God is known to us in this world, in the revelation of himself in creation, in the salvation history of Israel, and ultimately in God made visible in Jesus. Worship-prayer focuses on God's self-giving love through which he recapitulates the human condition, restores our union with God, and promises a restored creation in the new heavens and new earth. This history that we pray is not dead but alive and active for it is God's activity, God's presence, God's reality working within history to redeem it and restore it.

Second, we must remember that *the prayer of worship is done, not with the language we mortals create, but with the language of God.* Worship-prayer does God's history in this world using the language that is particular and peculiar to the Christian story. The language of prayer is the language of creation, fall, covenant, Passover, tabernacle, prophetic utterance, incarnation, death, resurrection, ascension, church, baptism, Eucharist, eternal intercession, eschaton. These words are necessary because they speak God's voice and presence. They are not common to the other religions of the world, nor are they generic. They are the specific words of

163

the biblical God, and consequently they constitute the language of worship, prayer, contemplation, and participation. There are no comparable words, no substitutes, no adaptations. The relationship between God and humanity must be articulated with these words for they constitute the language of Christian contemplation and participation.

Third, the contemplation that we do is *situated in this story and in the language of prayer that discloses this story.* There is a security and stability about the language of prayer that regulates our contemplation. Contemplation does not proceed out of an inner language that we create in the depths of our own person, as if we have the capacity to form and establish our own personal contemplation detached from the prayer of the church. Because the church prays God's story in the language of God's voice, our contemplation is always anchored in the public voice of the church. Our personal contemplation is dependent on the faithfulness of the church to articulate for us what we can only say in a fumbling way.

Yet the personal praying of the public prayers of the church is a necessary component of our contemplation. The public prayer is the bridge to the personal prayer. There is a process through which this prayer takes place. Augustine refers to that process as *Memoria—Intellectus—Voluntas.*[5] First, the prayer of the church makes an impression upon your mind. We recall through memory the particular story of God and the world. The story itself grasps our intellect, envelops it, overwhelms it with wonder and astonishment (contemplation), and then produces within us the determination of the will to find our place within that story and to let that story define the meaning of the self, of human existence in the world, of human history, of the cosmos. The story urges us to enter into its historical flow, to find our personal meaning within the larger story of the world, especially in the climax of world history in Jesus Christ and to now live in the world in him who shows us the fullness of human meaning. Now the will is engaged as we act (participation) as the continuation of Jesus in the world; the affections become engaged and we love as Jesus loved. We experience what Gregory of Nyssa alluded to: "If therefore these things be in you, God is indeed in you."[6]

Yet there is one more matter to consider. In the prayer of the church that does the saving acts of God in history, it is not the acts of God that constitute contemplation. Contemplation is the wonder and astonishment of the God who reveals his nature through these saving actions. What more astonishing thing could one say: "God has become incarnate, suffered for us, and is risen for us to reclaim us and the world to himself." We marvel in the kind of glorious God whose overwhelming love leads to these actions that reveal his very nature. And our nature, lifted up into the nature of Jesus, is now through him united to God and changed, transformed, and transfigured into the original nature created in the image of God. What wondrous splendor is the prayer of the church that we contemplate and through which we are stimulated by the Spirit to live in God's narrative.

Summary

I began this chapter by speaking to the current crisis of prayer in our worship. The major problem is that worship is no longer understood or practiced as praying God's story of the world. We have followed the culture of communication and "program" worship, or we make worship into a form of "presentation."

It is a paradigm shift to think and then to practice all of worship as a prayer in which we actually lift God's own story up to him as a prayer. I don't doubt that some congregations pray their songs. I have been in communities, especially liturgical charismatic, Pentecostal, and contemporary, where the congregation gets lost in praise and wonder. For many of these congregations worship is described as singing. I have pointed out, however, that the ancient church saw *all* of worship, from beginning to end, as the lifting up to God his own story in praise and thanksgiving. This is the shift that requires a new or, rather, old way of worshiping. In worship we do God's story as the prayer of God and his church for the whole world. Instead of creating our own feeble prayers, we use God's language of prayer and God's voice of prayer to lift up Jesus Christ, the ultimate prayer of the world and all that is within it.

Conclusion

My Journey toward an Ancient-Future Worship

*I*t is my intention that *Ancient-Future Worship* not only be read but also and especially be *applied*. Many books that are academic in nature are read for knowledge but not always for use. From the beginning of this project I have wanted the response to this book to be, "I can use this material in my church."

What Is an Ancient-Future Church?

Over the past years people have written or called me and said, "I want to visit an ancient-future church. Where can I go?" I don't usually have an answer because I don't think an ancient-future church or ancient-future worship is the next trend or that "cool" church over there. Ancient-future worship is not a gimmick or show or the latest adventure. There has been far too much "we need to start the church all over again" innovation since the late sixties. The church and its theology are not to be reinvented every generation. The church may need to be inspired, perhaps contextualized, but never trashed to start again.

God instituted the church on the day of Pentecost, and even though it has grown like a bramble bush with numerous branches, there is only one trunk and one set of roots that go back to God's involvement in history authoritatively recorded in Scripture. There is also that common core of universal teachings established in the early centuries of the faith, such as the Apostles' Creed and the Nicene Creed. My call is to help us recover these common roots of faith and worship. For these traditions have been received from the apostles and handed down in the church for centuries. So if you want a definition of ancient-future worship, it is this: *the common tradition of the church's worship in Word, Table, and song, practiced faithfully and communicated clearly in every context of the world.*

What stands at the very center of worship is Word and sacrament, through which God's vision for the world is proclaimed and enacted. What contextualizes this worship more than anything else is its music. Music is the vehicle that communicates worship in the language of the people. Music is also the vehicle of our personal response to the story of God's work in history. We also proclaim God's story in hymn and song, but nowhere in Scripture or in the history of the church have hymns and songs ever been held as a replacement for Word and Table. Word and Table remain the God-ordained way to remember God's saving deeds in history and anticipate his final triumph over death and all that is evil. So if you want to do ancient-future worship, learn God's story and do it in Word and Table and use hymns and songs for responses not only from the great treasury of the church through the centuries but also from music that is current.

Rediscover the Framework of God's Story

My journey toward the ancient framework of God's story began in the early seventies. I had been asked by the Slavic Gospel Mission in Wheaton to teach a course on Eastern theology in their missionary school. Even though I was teaching at Wheaton and had finished my doctorate in historical theology, I knew virtually nothing about the Eastern church fathers (the real cradle of early Christianity and the most influential thinkers in preserving the biblical content in the universal creeds of the church). So I spent the summer prior to my fall teaching assignment reading up on the Eastern Church.

At that time there were very few books available in the English language on the Eastern Church. Since then the Eastern Church has become more prominent in Western Protestant circles, and there are many conferences and books on the Eastern church fathers and their decisive influence on the development of the common tradition of Christian theology.

Secondary Writings

Fortunately for me, a new book had just been written by John Meyendorff, an Eastern theologian who taught at Fordham University in New York. The book, *Byzantine Theology*,[1] was printed in a limited edition of one thousand copies, evidently because the publisher was skeptical about its possible sales. I paid $19.95 for the book, which at that time (1974) was astronomical for a book of its size. (The book is still in print and has sold thousands.) Little did I know that I was about to begin a journey that to this day is not finished.

Byzantine Theology is divided into two parts. The first part is an introduction to the history of the Eastern Church. The second is an introduction to the theology of Eastern thought. It was the theological section that blew me away. The most decisive impact made on my heart was the paradigm of *creation–incarnation–re-creation.* These three words capture the basic framework of biblical and ancient church thinking. The previous paradigm I used to interpret God's story was derived from my Western training: creation–sin–redemption, which was introduced by Augustine, the shaper of Western thought. The same theme was continued by Calvin and was handed down to evangelicals during the Enlightenment. It still prevails today as the major way of thinking about the Bible as a whole.

There is nothing wrong with the Western model itself. The problem is the way it has been interpreted and applied. The popular approach, at least in my background, is to place the accent on sin in its personal and moral dimensions, thus not dealing adequately with the principalities and powers. Augustine, medieval theologians, and Calvin, as well as evangelicals, have placed a great deal of emphasis on personal sin, the need for confession, and personal appropriation of the death of Christ as a sacrifice for our sin. This emphasis led the West to a nearly exclusive concentration on the sacrificial view of the atonement without a strong connection to the resurrection and to the triumph of Jesus over sin, death, and the powers of evil. The exclusive preoccupation with the satisfaction theory of the cross has failed to adequately see the unity that exists between creation, the incarnation, and ultimately the restoration of all God's creation. It fosters instead an individualistic form of Christianity.

As I read *Byzantine Theology* (over and over again, mulling it in my mind and heart), I realized that the missing link in Western theology is a deep appreciation for the incarnation and subsequent *Christus Victor* theme of how God incarnate won a victory over sin and death. For example, in the West many seem stumped by the virgin birth. We believe in the miraculous conception, but we are not sure what to do with it. Not so with the Eastern fathers. They know exactly what to do with the incarnation. God in the womb of the Virgin Mary united with his entire creation in order to reverse the fallenness of creature and creation by taking into his own body the consequence of sin, which is death. Jesus, as the second Adam, defeated all sin and death that originated with the first Adam. Just as the first Adam affects all creation because of his sin, so also the second Adam rescues all creation because of his righteousness. In death Jesus defeats death. In his resurrection he begins a new act of creation that will ultimately be fulfilled in his second coming. In the meantime he ascended to the Father, where he now continually intercedes on behalf of the world and rules until all his enemies are under his feet. As Paul has written to the Philippians, "Every tongue [will] confess that Jesus Christ is Lord" (Phil. 2:11).

Eastern thought is wonderfully captured in another book I was introduced to at about the same time—*Christus Victor*, by Gustaf Aulen.[2] Aulen effectively argues that *Christus Victor* was the primary atonement view of the early church fathers (this view does not in any way deny the sacrifice of Christ). The book contains a splendid chapter on how Irenaeus develops *Christus Victor*. (All the ancient liturgies pray the *Christus Victor* theme; see chapter 4.) Aulen also writes a revealing chapter on the shift in medieval theology where the *Christus Victor* theme was dropped in favor of an exclusive emphasis on the sacrifice of Christ. You can see that shift in the Roman Mass, parts of which appear in chapter 4.

As I continued my studies in Eastern thought, I came across other names and books that helped me with my growing passion

170

for the ancient framework of creation–incarnation–re-creation. There were only a few of these books that I have read and reread, the most helpful being Georges Florovsky, *Creation and Redemption*.[3] Florovsky, professor of Eastern Church history at Harvard University, simply took me deeper and deeper into the ancient church fathers. His mastery of the fathers and ability to bring them together broadened my appreciation of the ancient framework of Scripture. It opened a new world for me and taught me how to read the fathers of the church.

Another secondary book on the ancient framework of Christianity that I recommend is by a brilliant young theologian, David Bentley Hart, who has taught at Duke, among other places. What I appreciate about his book, *The Beauty of the Infinite*,[4] is not only his knowledge of the fathers and their framework for interpreting God's story but also the way in which he brings the fathers into conversation with postmodern philosophers and our post-Christian cultural setting. He, along with others, like N. T. Wright, see that our era has affinities with the Roman era. The issues we must deal with today include widespread war, the breakdown of morality, and pluralism of philosophy and religion (especially Gnosticism). Just as the fathers interacted with powers and principalities of their time, so also we must interact with the powers and principalities of our time. In order to confront the powers of our day, we would do well to recover the ancient framework of Scripture and restore the emphasis on *Christus Victor*.

After the church settled into Christendom during the medieval era, they believed the cultural setting was transformed, resulting in the shift in emphasis from *Christus Victor* to the exclusive concentration on the sacrifice interpretation of the atonement. Both Florovsky and Hart show us the way to recover the ancient creation–incarnation–re-creation framework and resurrect *Christus Victor* in the midst of the postmodern, post-Christian, and neo-pagan era in which we live.

Primary Writings

It may seem strange to you that I began with secondary writings and only now take you to the primary sources. There are people who are conceptual and need to see the big picture before they look at the details. Others prefer to start with the details and eventually get to the big picture. I need to see things whole. Then I can make more sense out of the pieces of the puzzle. So I often read secondary books that give me the "lay of the land"; then I pursue topics of interest in the primary sources.

I was first introduced to the fathers of the second century in a graduate course on the apostolic fathers (so called because they are the defenders of the apostolic tradition). This course centered around the authenticity of the manuscripts and the meaning of disputed Greek words. The course did not deal with the theology of these second-century figures. However, because I read the ancient fathers, I developed an interest in the link between the apostles of the New Testament and their immediate successors and interpreters.

One of the most helpful books linking the first and second centuries was Cyril C. Richardson, *Early Christian Fathers*.[5] I read with great interest the seven letters of Ignatius, bishop of Antioch in AD 110, the Didache, and especially *Against Heresies* by Irenaeus, bishop of Lyons. These writers along with other fathers of the second century (Clement, Justin Martyr, Tertullian) opened windows to the world of the second century. I was introduced to the second-century Christian struggling to preserve the apostolic faith. Here was a world where Christians were martyred for their faith and leaders struggled with Gnostic heresies. Here numerous pagans were converted to Christ and the church. Here the church developed the catechumenate to teach new converts how to think and live as Christians.

I cannot begin to tell you how formative these second-century fathers and documents have been in making my own paradigm shift from modernity to a more story-formed understanding of God's work in history. There is much I could say about these writings, but I will limit myself to the most important theologian of the second century, Irenaeus. I have developed his steadfast commitment to apostolic truth in *Ancient-Future Faith*,[6] so I will only make a few limited comments here on only one of his themes—the theology of recapitulation (based on Ephesians 1:10, "To bring all things in heaven and on earth together under one head, even Christ").

The theology of recapitulation is another way of describing the ancient framework of God's story: creation–incarnation–re-creation.

Recapitulation brings together the first Adam and the second Adam themes of Paul. It brings together all the typologies of Scripture and emphasizes the whole of Scripture, refusing to compartmentalize this or that doctrine or teaching without its connection to everything else. Jesus Christ is the new Adam who *does it over again*. He sums up the history of the world. He triumphs over death and all that is evil, winning the world back for his heavenly Father, returning it to the garden of God's glory. This same Lord rules over creation forever in his kingdom.

I gradually began to grasp the significance of recapitulation. When I did, I read Scripture with new eyes, seeing everything whole. Events were connected; the stories of Israel were understood anew; the Gospels, especially the words of Jesus about the powers, took on a new life. I found everywhere in the Epistles, especially in Paul, a theology of God's Triune activity in all of history. Everything centered around Christ. Paul's writings took on new life.

A central motif of recapitulation is the incarnation. Incarnational thinking is all through Scripture and central to Ignatius, Irenaeus, and Tertullian (to name a few). However, theories of the incarnation began to take on form in the late third and early fourth centuries. One presbyter, Arius, spread the view that the Word, which became incarnate, was not God but God's first act of creation. Arius taught that the incarnate Word was not of the same essence as the Father. He was God's first-formed (begotten) creature, sent to save the world. He was God's appointed Redeemer, but he was not, Arius claimed, of the same essence or substance as God the Father.

His opponent was Athanasius, the great theologian of the fourth century and defender of the incarnation. Athanasius argued that the incarnate Word was not a creature *made* by God but was the incarnation of God himself. The Word of God incarnate is God himself united with creature and creation in the womb of the Virgin Mary. In his seminal work, *On the Incarnation*,[7] Athanasius goes to the heart of the matter—if God himself in his own nature and substance did not become incarnate, united to our humanity, *then God did not save us*. It was the Athanasian doctrine that won the day at the Council of Nicea. And today when we recite the Nicene Creed, we confess that the incarnate Word of God is not made but eternally begotten of God himself. So it is God of very God

173

who became incarnate and saved us. This is a major principle of ancient theology—*only God saves*. Here is that crucial section of the Nicene Creed confessing the incarnate Word to be of the same essence of the Father:

> We believe in one Lord, Jesus Christ,
>   the only Son of God,
>   *eternally begotten of the Father,*
>   *God from God, Light from Light,*
>   *true God from true God,*
>   *begotten, not made,*
>   *of one Being with the Father.*
>   Through him all things were made.
>   For us and for our salvation
>   he came down from heaven:
>   by the power of the Holy Spirit
>   he became incarnate from the Virgin Mary,
>   and was made man.
>   For our sake he was crucified under Pontius Pilate;
>   he suffered death and was buried.
>   On the third day he rose again
>   in accordance with the Scriptures;
>   he ascended into heaven
>   and is seated at the right hand of the Father.
>   He will come again in glory to judge the *living and the dead*,
>   and his kingdom will have no end.[8]

What was missing in my education and in my background was a theology of recapitulation. Rediscovering these ancient fathers and exposure to their framework of creation—incarnation—re-creation led me to a deeper evangelical faith. I have a better understanding of what I had glibly confessed all my life. All my life I had heard words such as, "Let God in your life," "Give God a chance," "Accept him as your Savior and you will discover the rich meaning of life." I gradually began to understand that these phrases and others like them turn the gospel inside out. I once understood the gospel as God asking me to let him into my narrative, to find room for him in my heart and life. But now I realize that God bids me to find my place in his narrative. In God's story, he, with his own two hands—the incarnate Word and the Holy Spirit—recapitulated and reversed the human situation so I can now live in him. Through him I can live in the expectation of a restored world without the presence of evil. Here and now, because God became incarnate and recapitulated all things, I live in him, in his narrative, and he lives in my life, which is to be a witness to his narrative for the world.

The Story of God

I do not remember exactly when I began to think clearly about the story of the entire world as the story of God. It grew along with my reading and contemplation and especially with the two years of intense thinking I did to write *The Divine Embrace*.[9] In this writing the ancient paradigm of thinking gained new clarity in my mind and a burning conviction in my heart. This deep appreciation for reading Scripture as divine narrative culminated in the preparation of *A Call to an Ancient Evangelical Future* (see appendix).

But let us step back into the early church fathers. What primary sources did I read that connected the framework of creation–incarnation–re-creation with the story of God?

I have to begin again with Irenaeus, the giant of second-century Christian thinkers. As I read Irenaeus and others I saw God's narrative much differently than the liberal version popularized in the seventies and eighties. Liberals really did not want to own the historical, earthy nature of the story. So they invented catchwords to affirm the story but deny its historical nature: The story is a myth. Jesus is the universal mono-myth. It was all summed up in the phrase, "the Jesus of history, and the Christ of faith." There is a difference, they said. You can deny the union of the Creator with his creatures and creation as *actually* happening yet affirm it as the universal truth of all religious experience. This view is a new kind of Gnosticism that needs to be rejected today as soundly as Irenaeus rejected the Gnosticism of his own day. (There is no need to prove the historicity of the narrative. It is simply accepted as the authoritative and inspired record of God's saving deeds and revealed commentary.)

Irenaeus's version of narrative is based not on myth but historical fact: The story of God really happened in time, space, and history.

God created this very material world. God became involved in world history in Israel and, of course, became incarnate to change the direction of the world. And Christ will physically return to re-create this earthly home. The mandate of creation for humanity to live in God's will and to make the earth a dwelling for his glory will literally and really be fulfilled in the new heavens and new earth.

Sometimes when I tell people the ancient fathers took a story-formed approach to faith and Scripture, they smirk or raise an eyebrow as if to say, "You're making it up because that is the way you want it to be." I usually shrug my shoulders and smile, knowing that they have probably never read the fathers. However, what I should do (and have done on occasion) is encourage them to at least read Irenaeus, *On the Apostolic Preaching*. Then they will see how the early church fathers followed God's story recorded in Scripture.

On the Apostolic Preaching presents the story from beginning to end; Irenaeus thinks of it as a whole. In the introduction to Irenaeus's book, John Behr writes, "Irenaeus takes us effortlessly through a demonstration of the apostolic preaching concerning the activity of God from creation to the exaltation of Son." In the preface to the book, Irenaeus makes the historicity of God's story clear by saying that we are to "believe what really is, as it is."[10]

Irenaeus is the first father of the second century to have the full Scripture at his disposal, and he approaches Scripture as the authoritative Word of God that provides us with a panoramic view of history. *On the Apostolic Preaching* begins with creation, the fall, and the history of humanity through Israel. Then the book deals with God's rescue in Jesus Christ, the incarnate Word of God. Irenaeus uses intertextual arguments to demonstrate the truth of the story presented. He draws particularly from prophecy, as do other previous writers such as Ignatius (AD 110) and Justin Martyr (AD 150). According to Behr, "Irenaeus demonstrates that there is but one God who has made Himself known through His one Son, Jesus Christ, by the one Holy Spirit, to the one human race, bringing his creatures made from mud into the intimacy of communion with Himself."[11] Indeed, we can sing and preach with confidence that God has recapitulated the error of the first-formed man by the obedience of the second-formed man. By his own two hands—the incarnate

Word and Holy Spirit—he has renewed the face of the earth, and we can now live in hope and expectation of God's completed history.

The theme of recapitulation is central to other writings from the second century. A case in point is the first full sermon of the Christian tradition. That sermon, which I refer to in chapter 5, is *On Pascha*, the Easter sermon by Melito of Sardis, written and preached about AD 195. Because I have already referred to this work, I will mention it only in passing as a sermon that gives us insight on how central the story of Israel and the story of Jesus are to preaching and communicating the gospel in the ancient church. It is full of imagery and typology—providing us with a powerful example of how to preach the biblical text in a story-formed way today.

Preaching, of course, is what we do in worship. We proclaim God's story, remembering his mighty deeds of salvation. In the Eucharist we enact or dramatize God's story and its anticipated future, and in doing so, we are actually ushered into God's kingdom in a momentary, existential experience of the kingdom to come.

Another ancient work that has influenced the history of both Eastern and Western liturgy is Hippolytus's *On the Apostolic Tradition*, written about AD 215.[12] This work has been mentioned previously, so I will only make a few comments here—and these comments refer only to the narrative nature of the eucharistic prayer (*anaphora*). The story, of course, is Triune. Hippolytus demonstrates how the eucharistic prayer was directed in praise of the Father, in memory of the Son's work in history, and in anticipation of the Spirit's work of uniting God's people into one and confirming God's truth in faith (see the section on Hippolytus and the table titled "The Text of Hippolytus" in chapter 5).

Summary

I have given you a brief insight into a few of the more important primary and secondary works that have helped me make the journey out of the modern way of thinking to the more Hebraic and holistic ancient way of thinking.

My journey does not present a norm for others. There are, I am sure, many who have traveled from modernity to an ancient way of thinking via a different route. However, I hope that my journey will help you as your heart and mind are increasingly inclined toward the theology and practice of the early church.

In sum, I have been learning and continue to learn how to spiritually read the paradigm of creation–incarnation–re-creation through this "old way," the story-formed hermeneutic of the faith—the story of how God recapitulates the world (creatures and creation) and wins it back to himself to fulfill all his creational purposes. Learning how to read Scripture spiritually prepares you to do ancient-future worship, a worship true to the apostolic tradition.

Appendix

A Call to an Ancient Evangelical Future

Prologue

In every age the Holy Spirit calls the Church to examine its faithfulness to God's revelation in Jesus Christ, authoritatively recorded in Scripture and handed down through the Church. Thus, while we affirm the global strength and vitality of worldwide Evangelicalism in our day, we believe the North American expression of Evangelicalism needs to be especially sensitive to the new external and internal challenges facing God's people.

These external challenges include the current cultural milieu and the resurgence of religious and political ideologies. The internal challenges include Evangelical accommodation to civil religion, rationalism, privatism and pragmatism. In light of these challenges, we call Evangelicals to strengthen their witness through a recovery of the faith articulated by the consensus of the ancient Church and its guardians in the traditions of Eastern Orthodoxy, Roman Catholicism, the Protestant Reformation and the Evangelical awakenings. Ancient Christians faced a world of paganism, Gnosticism and political domination. In the face of heresy and persecution, they understood history through Israel's story, culminating in the death and resurrection of Jesus and the coming of God's Kingdom.

Today, as in the ancient era, the Church is confronted by a host of master narratives that contradict and compete with the gospel. The pressing question is: who gets to narrate the world? The Call to an Ancient Evangelical Future challenges Evangelical Christians to restore the priority of the divinely inspired biblical story of God's acts in history. The narrative of God's Kingdom holds eternal implications for the mission of the Church, its theological reflection, its public ministries of worship and spirituality and its life in the world. By engaging these themes, we believe the Church will be strengthened to address the issues of our day.

1. On the Primacy of the Biblical Narrative

We call for a return to the priority of the divinely authorized canonical story of the Triune God. This story—Creation, Incarnation, and Re-creation—was effected by Christ's recapitulation of human history and summarized by the early Church in its Rules of Faith. The gospel-formed content of these Rules served as the key to the interpretation of Scripture and its critique of contemporary culture, and thus shaped the church's pastoral ministry. Today, we call Evangelicals to turn away from modern theological methods that reduce the gospel to mere propositions, and from contemporary pastoral ministries so compatible with culture that they camouflage God's story or empty it of its cosmic and redemptive meaning. In a world of competing stories, we call Evangelicals to recover the truth of God's Word as the story of the world, and to make it the centerpiece of Evangelical life.

2. On the Church, the Continuation of God's Narrative

We call Evangelicals to take seriously the visible character of the Church. We call for a commitment to its mission in the world in fidelity to God's mission (Missio Dei), and for an exploration of the ecumenical implications this has for the unity, holiness, catholicity, and apostolicity of the Church. Thus, we call Evangelicals to turn away from an individualism that makes the Church a mere addendum to God's redemptive plan. Individualistic Evangelicalism has contributed to the current problems of churchless Christianity, redefinitions of the Church according to business models, separatist ecclesiologies and judgmental attitudes toward the Church. Therefore, we call Evangelicals to recover their place in the community of the Church catholic.

3. On the Church's Theological Reflection on God's Narrative

We call for the Church's reflection to remain anchored in the Scriptures in continuity with the theological interpretation learned from the early Fathers. Thus, we call Evangelicals to turn away from methods that separate theological reflection from the common traditions of the Church. These modern methods compartmentalize God's story by analyzing its separate parts, while ignoring God's entire redemptive work as recapitulated in Christ. Anti-historical attitudes also disregard the common biblical and theological legacy of the ancient Church.

Such disregard ignores the hermeneutical value of the Church's ecumenical creeds. This reduces God's story of the world to one of many competing theologies and impairs the unified witness of the Church to God's plan for the history of the world. Therefore, we call Evangelicals to unity in "the tradition that has been believed everywhere, always and by all," as well as to humility and charity in their various Protestant traditions.

4. On the Church's Worship as Telling and Enacting God's Narrative

We call for public worship that sings, preaches and enacts God's story. We call for a renewed consideration of how God ministers to us in baptism, Eucharist, confession, the laying on of hands, marriage, healing and through the charisma of the Spirit, for these actions shape our lives and signify the meaning of the world. Thus, we call Evangelicals to turn away from forms of worship that focus on God as a mere object of the intellect or that assert the self as the source of worship. Such worship has resulted in lecture-oriented, music-driven, performance-centered and program-controlled models that do not adequately proclaim God's cosmic redemption. Therefore, we call Evangelicals to recover the historic substance of worship of Word and Table and to attend to the Christian year, which marks time according to God's saving acts.

5. On Spiritual Formation in the Church as Embodiment of God's Narrative

We call for a catechetical spiritual formation of the people of God that is based firmly on a Trinitarian biblical narrative. We are concerned when spirituality is separated from the story of God and baptism into the life of Christ and his Body. Spirituality, made independent from God's story, is often characterized by legalism, mere intellectual knowledge, an overly therapeutic culture, New Age Gnosticism, a dualistic rejection of this world and a narcissistic preoccupation with one's own experience. These false spiritualities are inadequate for the challenges we face in today's world. Therefore, we call Evangelicals to return to a historic spirituality like that taught and practiced in the ancient catechumenate.

6. On the Church's Embodied Life in the World

We call for a cruciform holiness and commitment to God's mission in the world. This embodied holiness affirms life, biblical morality and appropriate self-denial. It calls us to be faithful stewards of the created order and bold prophets to our contemporary culture. Thus, we call Evangelicals to intensify their prophetic voice against forms of indifference to God's gift of life, economic and political injustice, ecological insensitivity and the failure to champion the poor and marginalized. Too often we have failed to stand prophetically against the culture's captivity to racism, consumerism, political correctness, civil religion, sexism, ethical relativism, violence and the culture of death. These failures have muted the voice of Christ to the world through his Church and detract from God's story of the world, which the Church is collectively to embody. Therefore, we call the Church to recover its counter-cultural mission to the world.

Epilogue

In sum, we call Evangelicals to recover the conviction that God's story shapes the mission of the Church to bear witness to God's Kingdom and to inform the spiritual foundations of civilization. We set forth this Call as an ongoing, open-ended conversation. We are aware that we have our blind spots and weaknesses. Therefore, we encourage Evangelicals to engage this Call within educational centers, denominations and local churches through publications and conferences.

We pray that we can move with intention to proclaim a loving, transcendent, triune God who has become involved in our history. In line with Scripture, creed and tradition, it is our deepest desire to embody God's purposes in the mission of the Church through our theological reflection, our worship, our spirituality and our life in the world, all the while proclaiming that Jesus is Lord over all creation.[1]

Notes

Chapter 1 Worship *Does* God's Story

1. *The Book of Common Prayer* (New York: Seabury Press, 1979), 864.

Chapter 3 Worship *Anticipates* the Future

1. For an expansion of these themes see Samuel F. Balentine, *The Torah's Vision of Worship* (Minneapolis: Fortress Press, 1999). I am indebted to him for these insights.

2. Barb Stellwagen, personal email message to author, September 16, 2006.

3. G. K. Beale, *The Temple and the Church's Mission: A Biblical Theology of the Dwelling Place of God* (Downers Grove, IL: InterVarsity Press, 2004), 31.

4. Ibid., 32–33.

5. Ibid., 60.

6. Ibid., 48.

Chapter 4 How the *Fullness* of God's Story Became Lost

1. From the *Apostolic Constitutions*, book VII, 2–7, quoted in Lucien Deiss, ed., *Early Sources of the Liturgy*, 2nd ed., trans. Benet Weatherhead (Collegeville, MN: Liturgical Press, 1975), 154–55.

2. Ibid., 155–56.

3. John Warren Morris, "The Byzantine Liturgy (Ninth Century)," in *Twenty Centuries of Christian Worship*, ed. Robert Webber (Peabody, MA: Hendrickson, 1994), 163–64.

4. Michael S. Driscoll, "The Roman Catholic Mass (1520)," in ibid., 177–79.

5. Elsie McKee, "Calvin: *The Form of Church Prayers*, Strassburg Liturgy (1545)," in ibid., 202.

6. Dorrell Todd Marirna, "The Westminster Directory," in ibid., 230–31.

7. G. Thomas Halbrooks, "A Baptist Model of Worship," in ibid., 231–35.

Chapter 5 Worship

1. *The First Apology of Justin, the Martyr*, in *Early Christian Fathers*, ed. Cyril C. Richardson (Philadelphia: Westminster Press, 1953), 67, 287.

2. Irenaeus, *Against Heresies*, book III, 12, in ibid., 360, emphasis added.

3. Ibid., emphasis added.

4. Ibid., book IV, 2, 386.

5. Ibid.

6. Ibid., book IV, 12, 389–90.

7. Melito of Sardis, *On Pascha*, trans. Alistair Stewart-Sykes (Crestwood, NY: St. Vladimir's Seminary Press, 2001), 37.

8. Ibid., 37.

9. Ibid., 48.

10. Ibid., 52.

11. Ibid., 54.

12. Ibid., 56.

13. Ibid., 66.

14. Ibid., 34–37.

15. Hippolytus, *On the Apostolic Tradition*, intro. Alistair Stewart-Sykes (Crestwood, NY: St. Vladimir's Seminary Press).

16. R. C. D. Jasper and G. J. Cuming, eds., *Prayers of the Eucharist: Early and Reformed*, 3rd ed. (Collegeville, MN: Liturgical Press, 1990), 34–35.

Chapter 6 Word

1. Pastor Jason Snook, personal email message to author, fall 2006.

2. Pastor Dave Wiebe, personal email message to author, fall 2006.

3. St. Irenaeus of Lyons, *On the Apostolic Preaching*, trans. John Behr (Crestwood, NY: St. Vladimir's Seminary Press, 1997), 7.

4. Marvin R. Wilson, *Our Father Abraham: Jewish Roots of the Christian Faith* (Grand Rapids: Eerdmans, 1989), 137.

5. Ibid., 145.

Chapter 7 Eucharist

1. The student's name is withheld to protect his privacy.

2. Ignatius, *To the Trallians*, 9, in Cyril C. Richardson, ed., *Early Christian Fathers* (Philadelphia: Westminster, 1953), 100.

3. Ignatius, *To the Smyrneans*, 7, in ibid., 114.

4. Ignatius, *To the Trallians*, 2, in ibid., 99.

5. Ignatius, *To the Ephesians*, 13, in ibid., 91.

6. Ibid., 20, 93.

7. Ignatius, *To the Philadelphians*, 4, in ibid., 108.

8. Ignatius, *To the Romans*, 7, in ibid., 105.

9. Justin Martyr, *The First Apology of Justin, the Martyr*, in ibid., 286.

10. Pierre Teilhard de Chardin, *The Divine Milieu* (New York: Harper and Row, 1968), 66.

11. Jasper and Cuming, eds., *Prayers of the Eucharist*, 35.

12. Alexander Schmemann, *The Eucharist: Sacrament of the Kingdom* (Crestwood, NY: St. Vladimir's Press, 1988), 125.

Chapter 8 Prayer

1. Schmemann, *Eucharist*, 83.

2. The quotations of the St. John Chrysostom liturgy are taken from Morris, "The Byzantine Liturgy," in *Twenty Centuries of Christian Worship*, ed. Webber, 152–71.

3. Gregory of Nyssa, Homily 10, *On the Song of Songs*, cited by Charles Kannengiesen, "The Spiritual Message of the Great Fathers," in *Christian Spirituality*, ed. Bernard McGinn and John Meyendorff (New York: Crossroad, 1986), 74.

4. Gregory of Nyssa, Homily 6, *On the Beatitudes*, in ibid., 72, 74.

5. Augustine, quoted in Hans Urs von Balthasar, *Prayer* (San Francisco: Ignatius Press, 1986), 133.

6. Gregory of Nyssa, *On the Beatitudes*, in *Christian Spirituality*, ed. McGinn and Meyendorff, 74.

Conclusion

1. John Meyendorff, *Byzantine Theology: Historical Trends and Doctrinal Themes* (New York: Fordham University Press, 1974).

2. Gustaf Aulen, *Christus Victor: A Historical Study of the Three Main Ideas of the Atonement* (New York: Macmillan, 1969; Eugene, OR: Wipf & Stock, 2003).

3. Georges Florovsky, *Creation and Redemption* (Belmont, MA: Nordland Publishing, 1976).

4. David Bentley Hart, *The Beauty of the Infinite* (Grand Rapids: Eerdmans, 2003).

5. Cyril C. Richardson, ed., *Early Christian Fathers* (Philadelphia: Westminster, 1953).

6. Robert E. Webber, *Ancient-Future Faith* (Grand Rapids: Baker, 1999).

7. Athanasius, *On the Incarnation (De Incarnatione Verbi Dei)*, trans. and ed. a religious of C.S.M.V. (Crestwood, NY: St. Vladimir's Seminary Press, 1975).

8. *The Book of Common Prayer*, 358–59, emphasis added.

9. Robert E. Webber, *The Divine Embrace* (Grand Rapids: Baker, 2006).

10. St. Irenaeus of Lyons, *On the Apostolic Preaching*, trans. John Behr (Crestwood, NY: St. Vladimir's Seminary Press, 1997), 17.

11. Ibid., back cover.

12. Hippolytus, *On the Apostolic Tradition*.

Appendix

1. A Call to an Ancient Evangelical Future, © Northern Seminary 2006, Robert Webber and Phil Kenyon. Permission is granted to reproduce the Call in unaltered form with proper citation. To read and sign the Call, go to www.ancientfutureworship .com or www.aefcall.org.

This Call is issued in the spirit of *sic et non*; therefore those who affix their names to this Call need not agree with all its content. Rather, its consensus is that these are issues to be discussed in the tradition of *semper reformanda* as the church faces the new challenges of our time. Over a period of seven months, more than three hundred persons have participated via email to write the Call. These men and women represent a broad diversity of ethnicity and denominational affiliation. The four theologians who most consistently interacted with the development of the Call have been named as theological editors. The board of reference was given the special assignment of overall approval.

Selected Bibliography

Works Cited

Athanasius. *On the Incarnation (De Incarnatione Verbi Dei).* Translated and edited by a religious of C.S.M.V., with an introduction by C. S. Lewis. Crestwood, NY: St. Vladimir's Seminary Press, New Edition, 1975.

Aulen, Gustaf. *Christus Victor: A Historical Study of the Three Main Ideas of the Atonement.* New York: Macmillan, 1969; Eugene, OR: Wipf & Stock, 2003.

Balentine, Samuel E. *The Torah's Vision of Worship.* Minneapolis: Fortress Press, 1999.

Balthasar, Hans Urs von. *Prayer.* San Francisco: Ignatius, 1986.

Beale, G. K. *The Temple and the Church's Mission: A Biblical Theology of the Dwelling Place of God.* Downers Grove, IL: InterVarsity Press, 2004.

Deiss, Lucien. *Early Sources of the Liturgy.* 2nd ed. Trans. Benet Weatherhead. Collegeville, MN: Liturgical Press, 1975.

Florovsky, Georges. *Creation and Redemption.* Belmont, MA: Nordland Publishing, 1976.

Hart, David Bentley. *The Beauty of the Infinite.* Grand Rapids: Eerdmans, 2003.

Hippolytus. *On the Apostolic Tradition.* An English version with introduction and commentary by Alistair Stewart-Sykes. Crestwood, NY: St. Vladimir's Seminary Press, 2001.

St. Irenaeus of Lyons. *On the Apostolic Preaching.* Translation and introduction by John Behr. Crestwood, NY: St. Vladimir's Seminary Press, 1997.

Melito of Sardis. *On Pascha.* Translated, introduced, and annotated by Alistair Stewart-Sykes. Crestwood, NY: St. Vladimir's Seminary Press, 2001.

Meyendorff, John. *Byzantine Theology: Historical Trends and Doctrinal Themes.* New York: Fordham University Press, 1974.

Richardson, Cyril C., ed. and trans. *Early Christian Fathers.* Philadelphia: Westminster, 1953.

Schmemann, Alexander. *The Eucharist: Sacrament of the Kingdom.* Crestwood, NY: St. Vladimir's Seminary Press, 1988.

Webber, Robert E. *Twenty Centuries of Christian Worship.* Peabody, MA: Hendrickson, 1994.

Wilson, Marvin R. *Our Father Abraham.* Grand Rapids: Eerdmans, 1989.

Recommended Works

Anderson, Bernard A. *From Creation to New Creation*. Minneapolis: Fortress Press, 1994.

Baker, Jonny, and Doug Gay with Jenny Brown. *Alternative Worship*. Grand Rapids: Baker, 2004.

Bartholomew, Craig R., and Michael W. Goheen. *The Drama of Scripture*. Grand Rapids: Baker, 2004.

Basden, Paul. *Exploring the Worship Spectrum*. Grand Rapids: Zondervan, 2004.

Batson, David. *The Treasure Chest of the Early Christian*. Grand Rapids: Eerdmans, 2001.

Chan, Simon. *Liturgical Theology*. Downers Grove, IL: InterVarsity Press, 2006.

Church, Forester F., and Terrence J. Mulry, eds. *Earliest Christian Prayers*. New York: Macmillan, 1988.

Daley, Brian E. *The Hope of the Early Church*. Peabody: Hendrickson, 2003.

Dawson, John David. *Christian Figural Reading and the Fashioning of Identity*. Berkley: University of California Press, 2002.

Green, Joel B., and Michael Pasquarello III. *Narrative Reading, Narrative Preaching*. Grand Rapids: Baker, 2003.

Hall, Christopher A. *Learning Theology with the Church Fathers*. Downers Grove, IL: InterVarsity Press, 2002.

———. *Reading Scripture with the Church Fathers*. Downers Grove, IL: InterVarsity Press, 1988.

Lee, Philip J. *Against the Protestant Gnostics*. New York: Oxford, 1987.

Peterson, Eugene H. *Eat This Book*. Grand Rapids: Eerdmans, 2006.

Ramsey, Boniface. *Beginning to Read the Fathers*. New York: Paulist Press, 1985.

Seitz, Christopher R. *Figured Out*. Louisville: Westminster John Knox Press, 2001.

———, ed. *Nicene Christianity*. Grand Rapids: Brazos Press, 2001.

Thompson, Bard. *Liturgies of the Western World*. New York: World Publishing, 1962.

Webber, Robert E. *Ancient-Future Faith*. Grand Rapids: Baker, 1999.

———. *The Divine Embrace*. Grand Rapids: Baker, 2006.

———. *Worship Old and New*. Grand Rapids: Zondervan, 2nd ed., 1994.

Wilken, Robert L. *Remembering the Christian Past*. Grand Rapids: Eerdmans, 1995.

Williams, D. H. *Retrieving the Tradition and Renewing Evangelicalism*. Grand Rapids: Eerdmans, 1999.

———, ed. *The Free Church and the Early Church*. Grand Rapids: Eerdmans, 2002.

———, ed. *Tradition, Scripture and Interpretation*. Grand Rapids: Baker, 2006.

Index